HANDBOOK OF

WHISKY

Handbook of

Whisky

Dave Broom

A complete guide
to the world's best malts,
blends and brands

hamlyn

CONTENTS

Commissioning Editor: Nina Sharman
Copy-editor: Adrian Tempany
Editor: Tarda Davison-Aitkins
Executive Art Editor: Leigh Jones
Design: Ian Muggeridge
Picture Research: Rosie Garai
Production Controller: Louise Hall

First published in Great Britain in 2000
by Hamlyn, an imprint of Octopus Publishing Group
Limited
2–4 Heron Quays, London E14 2JP

Copyright © 2000 Octopus Publishing Group Limited

ISBN 0 600 60491 8

A catalogue record for this book is available from the
British Library

Produced by Toppan
Printed in China

INTRODUCTION

'We'd left the empty casks out in the sun, because that allows all the whisky that is soaked into the wood to come out. After a couple of days we'd tip the whisky into a bucket. Now, one day, this chap was doing just that when he saw the manager coming round the corner. He panicked and dropped the cask on his foot, but he couldn't report it as an accident because in two days' time we were having a dinner to celebrate 2,000 days accident free! He hobbled around until after the dinner and immediately went to hospital.'

The old distillery worker was in fits of laughter, recounting outrageous stories about the good old days in Scotland, when men were given three huge drams of new make a day and still felt it their moral duty to steal more from under the noses of management or Customs and Excise. Every old worker has a fund of tales, painting a picture of an industry which would mortify today's corporate management – but an industry alive with a wild, vital human warmth.

It was Bowmore's Jim McEwan who first said to me: 'Remember, it is people who make whisky,' yet few books have sought to distil this human element. Whisky – whether from Scotland, Ireland or North America – has been sold as a brand, almost as an industrial product, which seems to spring mysteriously from the still into the bottle. Does its production have more to do with fairies and alchemy than with people?

My aim was to locate these shadowy folk and draw them into the glare of a whisky-loving world. This isn't a tour round every distillery or a tasting guide to every bottle; there are books which do that already. This is an insight into the characters responsible for a spirit currently in fine health – there are now more great whiskies on the market than at any other time in history.

As my research progressed it became clear that tracking down the talent would be difficult. The days of 50 people working at a distillery have long gone. Some are now run by one man. People are disappearing, computer screens are replacing hand valves and intuitive skills. Now that Ireland and Canada have proved that one distillery can

ABOVE *Empty casks of whisky sitting in the sun at Laphroaig, Scotland.*

produce a mass of brands, the industry is at a crossroads.

So, how will the computer age be reconciled with the legacy of traditional manpower? There are passionate advocates on both sides of the fence, although to reduce the debate to 'computers bad, hand-crafted good' is naïve and simplistic. Much may depend on corporate culture, but if you appear to take control away from the men who made your award-winning 20-year-old whisky, then what message are you sending out? Computerisation won't necessarily drive historic skills out of the system, but in some quarters it may signify an unhealthy cultural overhaul.

At the start of the 21st century, the whisky industry finds itself in the same situation as wine and beer at the end of the 20th century. Wine went through a stage of mechanisation and an eschewal of 'traditional' skills. Today the talk is of balancing technology with terroir and of 'hands-on' wine making. Brewers also brought in technology, which turned beer into a mass-produced

commodity, but the public demanded choice and triggered an explosion in hands-on microbreweries. A balance was struck.

How whisky copes with the same challenge is the question now on many people's lips.

Star rating

*	Average.
* *	Decent, if simple.
* * *	Very good.
* * * *	Excellent.
* * * * *	Simply the best.

Tasting, no matter how analytical, is inevitably a highly personal activity. Take the marks above as guides, not as decrees fixed in stone. Whisky, at the end of the day, is made to be enjoyed. Do so!

Note:
Whisky is spelt differently around the world: whisky is the usual spelling in the United Kingdom and Canada, while in Ireland and the United States the usual spelling is whiskey.
ABV (Alcohol by Volume) is 40% unless otherwise stated.

A POTTED HISTORY

It would be appropriate for a people-based profile of whisky to begin by naming the first whisky maker. Sadly, no-one knows who he was. In fact, no-one knows who the first distiller was. It is clear that from AD 4 onwards, alchemists in China, India, Arabia, Egypt and Greece were using distillation to make turpentine, medicines, makeup (*al-kohl*, our alcohol) and perfumes, but there is no evidence that they adapted brewing techniques to make whisky.

How the Irish and Scots got in on the act is equally mysterious. The Celts may have known about distillation, but apart from a couple of enigmatic references in the 6th century AD there's no proof. What is agreed is that distillation arrived in Scotland with the monks of the Celtic Church, suggesting that distillation was already taking place in Ireland – perhaps Irish monks had encountered the art in Sicily or Andalucia, or through their ancient trading links with the Phoenicians.

By the time Friar John Cor bought his famous eight bolls of malt in 1495 – the first record of whisky making in Scotland – distillation was widely practised across Europe. It is hardly surprising that the first distillers were monks: the water of life, *aquavitae* (*uisge beatha* in Scots Gaelic) was a medicine made in monastic laboratories, and markedly different to today's whisky. Flavoured with heather, honey, roots, herbs and spices – partly to hide off-flavours, partly because it was a medicine – this medieval mix was closer to a crude whisky liqueur.

Until the beginning of the 19th century the top Irish brands were flavoured in this way. It was only when whisky began to be made in great houses and crofts alike that it became recognisable as the drink we know today. Distillers have always used the main crop of their region as the base for their spirits, and in Scotland and Ireland that meant barley. Making whisky was a means of using up surplus grain: in winter, cattle could be fed on the grains left after mashing and crofters could use their whisky as part-payment of rent. Made in batches in small pot stills, the process used for malt whisky today, (see pages 12–13) whisky soon became an integral part of rural life.

When crofter-distillers from Scotland and Ireland were driven off their land from 1745 onwards, whisky spread to America and Canada. Though rye whiskey had been made as early as 1640, it was this sudden wave of immigrants that established whiskey as North America's spirit. They, too, used the local grains – rye, corn and wheat – and by 1783 commercial production had kicked off in Kentucky.

By 1825, the whisky industry in Scotland and Ireland was controlled by men of capital. Gone were the days of the crofter-distiller making enough to fuel the *craic* and the *ceilidh* and pay the rent. New legislation ushered in a building programme of new malt distilleries across the Highlands and in Ireland.

At the start of the 19th century Irish whiskey had the highest international reputation, with the heavily-peated Scottish malts considered an acquired taste. Then, in 1827, Robert Stein invented a continuous still (see pages 86–87), which not only made distilling less labour-intensive but produced a lighter, grain-based whisky which could be mass produced. Adapted in 1831 by Aeneas Coffey, the continuous still changed whisky production forever.

Distillers in the Scottish Lowlands seized the new invention and by the 1850s grocers and wine merchants such as John Walker, George Ballantine, James Chivas, John Dewar and Matthew Gloag began blending malt with the light grain, and the public sat up and took notice. The Irish resisted, for a time. Distillers including John Jameson and John Power, who were already enjoying international prestige with their pot-still whiskies, refused to use the continuous method, dismissing it as an adulteration of 'real' whisky.

The North Americans had no such qualms and Coffey's patent still was soon adopted in America and Canada. This interest, along with James Crow's research into quality control in Kentucky, improved

ABOVE *Copper is an essential ingredient in the making of fine whisky the world over.*

LEFT *Stone flagons were easy to transport – and easy to hide from the excise man.*

BOTTOM *Winston Churchill and James Stevenson from Johnnie Walker enjoy an chat.*

consistency. The Canadians were so enamoured of the Coffey still that, in 1875, they passed legislation decreeing that Canadian whisky could only be made from grain distilled in a continuous still, and aged for a minimum of three years in oak barrels. The quality-oriented, modern industry was taking shape.

Even at this stage there was no indication that whisky would become the world's best-selling spirit. Brandy was still more popular, but the vine parasite *phylloxera vastrix* put paid to that when, from the 1870s onwards, it wiped out Europe's vineyards – and the brandy industry with them.

It is entirely possible that American whiskey would have become the world's dominant player, were it not for the growth of the Temperance Movement in the US which led to Prohibition in 1919. At that time, Irish whiskey was selling more in America than Scotch, but while Scotch and Canadian whisky managed to retain a quality image, Irish whiskies lost their biggest market overnight and were being (badly) copied by bootleggers. Their reputation plummeted. At the same time, Irish independence led to the ban of Irish products in Britain and the Empire. With no markets left, the Irish industry imploded and blended Scotch took over.

This was the situation until the late 1970s when, either through industry complacency, or the inevitability of changing fashion, young drinkers turned away from brown spirits and the global whisky industry fell into deep depression. Blended Scotch has struggled hard to regain consumer confidence in its old markets, though it has enjoyed success in southern Europe and Asia. But in America, northern Europe and Britain, malts have kept the whisky dream alive. This recent fascination with premium whisky has also boosted the American whiskey industry and sparked a new optimism in Ireland and Canada. There are now more quality whiskies on offer than ever before, and a renewed interest in how they are made and the people who make them.

MAKING WHISKY

Every country has a different approach to making whisky, which will be discussed in detail at the beginning of each chapter. However, all are basically variations on the following rules.

Whisky is made from a cereal; some (or all) of it malted, that has been ground into a rough flour then mashed by passing hot water through the flour to extract a sweet liquid. This is cooled, yeast is added and the mixture ferments, turning into a crude beer. This is then distilled in either a pot or a column still. Because alcohol boils at a lower temperature than water, the alcohol vapours are released first. These are condensed into a clear, strong spirit which is then aged in oak casks.

Malt whisky is made exclusively from malted barley and is distilled twice (or occasionally three times) in pot stills. It is then aged in used oak casks for a minimum of three years.

Grain whisky is made from either corn or wheat, with some malted barley. It is distilled in a column still to produce a lighter spirit with a high degree of alcohol, and aged in used casks for a minimum of three years. Blended scotch is a combination of grain and malt whisky.

Irish whiskey can be made in a number of styles. Pure pot still, using malted and/or unmalted barley; a mix of pot and column still, and all column still. It, too, must be aged in used casks for three years.

American whiskey (bourbon) must be made from a minimum 51 per cent corn,

ABOVE *Pure water remains a vital ingredient.*

RIGHT *Peat gives whisky a distinctive smoky 'reek'.*

BELOW *Drying malted barley in a kiln.*

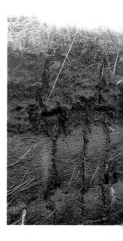

CLOCKWISE FROM BOTTOM LEFT *Fermenting to produce a crude beer; filling the still; getting ready to close the door and turn up the heat; under the watchful eye of the stillman.*

BELOW *Staving off the inevitable – wood contributes up to 60% of a whisky's flavour.*

to which can be added wheat, malted barley and rye. It is distilled in either a single column still, a column still with a second still called a 'doubler', or in pot stills. Tennessee whiskey must also be filtered through a bed of charcoal. All American produced whiskey must be aged in new charred-oak casks.

Canadian whisky is a blend of whiskies most commonly made in column stills from wheat, corn, barley and rye (either singly or combined), and must be aged for a minimum of three years in used oak casks. Canadian distillers are allowed to add up to 9.09 per cent of other mature spirits (Cognac, rum, bourbon, malt, sherry) to the final blend.

It is perhaps strange that a small wet country on the far northwest fringe of Europe should produce a cult drink that has captured the world's imagination. For 'cult' is the only way to describe single malt Scotch these days. It has crossed boundaries of class, age and sex: cherished by tweedy colonels and hipper-than-thou urbanites, malt has never had it so good.

It wasn't always like this. As recently as the mid-1970s few people had ever tasted a single malt. Scotch meant blends, and malt distilleries were simply the suppliers of fillings for the big brands. That in itself was a far cry from malt's rural beginnings.

Distilling was part of the Highland way of life and there was a pleasing rhythm to it.

SINGLE MALT SCOTCH

It was a way to use up surplus grain, the cattle could be fed on the draff and the excess production could be sold or bartered. The first signs of the modern malt industry emerged after the failure of the 1745 rebellion, when draconian laws effectively outlawed Highland culture. By restricting the production and sale of Highland malt, the government forced people off the land. Those who stayed were soon criminalized, as they were forced into illegal distillation and smuggling to make ends meet. A change in the law in 1823 paved the way for tenant farmers, landowners and entrepreneurs to take over production. Larger plants were built and, when blended whisky appeared in the 1850s, malt became part of a new-look industry. It's only now, as blends have fallen from favour, that single malt is able to shine.

Today, most malt drinkers regard single malt much as they regard fine wine – distilleries make regional specialities through their unique terroir, don't they? Well, regionality is a starting point, but that's all; if there is a Speyside style it is born from production and not terroir. If Mr Grant realized that Mr Smith was selling lots of whisky, isn't it likely that Mr Grant would try and make his whisky taste vaguely the same? There are exceptions, such as Islay, where the peat is different and malts matured in the island's sea-lashed warehouses will absorb some of the spume-laden air. But the beauty of Islay is that it never behaves in the same way as the rest of Scotland.

So what makes each malt a distinct individual? Water has a slight effect, particularly if it has run over peat and picked up phenolics. The type of malt used may also have an impact, though only two distillers insist on using one strain for its flavours. Even malting is a fairly standardized – if highly skilled – process. Flavour can appear here if peat is used in the kilning, but most modern malt is unpeated.

In most malts, flavour begins in the washbacks. If you ferment for less than 48 hours the spirit will have a nutty-spicy character; any longer and you start introducing more complex flavour compounds. Ultimately, though, it's down to the shape and size of the stills, the speed at which they are run, the size of the middle cut and how the vapour is condensed. The shape directs how the vapour rises up the neck, tall stills should produce a lighter spirit, as the heavier alcohols fail to make it up the neck. Conversely, short and fat stills should give a heavier result. The length of the cut will then affect character; the wider the cut, more rich, powerful congeners are collected and this is where peatiness lurks; while worm tubs tend to produce a meatier spirit than condensers.

Finally, there's the forgotten element – wood. Up to 60 per cent of a malt's flavour comes from the barrel, and each type of cask interacts with the new make spirit in a different way. A clever distiller can play as many tunes by blending wood types as he can with the stills. This is not to dismiss malt distilling as coldly scientific; the more you delve into its mysteries the more bizarre it becomes. The spirit of the spirit remains enigmatic, elusive, magical. Long may it remain so.

HIGHLAND PARK

Orkney is like no other part of Scotland: Second World War airfields lie next to pre-Celtic burial mounds, cathedrals close to stone circles, layered civilisations, ancient and modern. Orkney is in tune with its strange past and slightly fearful, like any remote community in these days of centralisation, of its future. There are echoes of this duality at Highland Park, which is tapping into old lore of whisky making while taking radical steps into the 21st century.

In the low light of a Y-shaped malt barn, Jimmy Shearer takes me on a vivid tour through the life of a grain of barley. He has been a maltman here for 30 years, and knows how many tons of malt he has steeped, turned, grubbed and fed into the kiln. The astounding 25-year-old malt was made with barley turned by Jimmy, which helps to put things into perspective.

The process of floor malting seems timeless, but there have been subtle changes. New varieties are appearing every year, and though most are tested, not all can stand up to the handling involved in floor malting,

where a thicker shell is required. Highland Park (like Laphroaig, Bowmore, Balvenie and Springbank) has retained this traditional method of making malt for some of its requirements. For Jimmy it has become second nature: checking the growth of the grain by splitting the husk grain between his nails and seeing how big the white spike of starch is; knowing when to turn the floor, how thick to lay it depending on the weather. As he says: 'If you don't get the growth right, you won't get good malt.' It seems complicated, so many little things can go wrong. 'If you worry about it, it's no use,' he says, dismissing that idea with a grin, but then he has been at it for 30 years.

Retaining the floor maltings is more than just a matter of pride, it is a fundamental part of the Highland Park profile. 'We like to think it's our barley that makes the difference' says Jimmy. 'We got some peated malt from somewhere else once and we didn't like it; it didn't work like our peated malt, it was coarser. We should stick with our own.'

And they do. 'The secret of Highland Park is that all the peated malt we use is floor-malted here and kilned over our own peat,' says manager Jim Robertson. 'The peat draws a huge influence from the heather. The fibrous stuff we use is full of heather roots – even the lower levels are permeated by roots. I'm sure that gives us that heather-honey influence.'

After this ultra-traditional welcome it comes as a surprise to find trials taking place in the stillroom with automatic cut control. It's a big change from stillman David Muir's early days. 'We used to have mirrors to see how high the wash still was rising and controlled the stills with steam valves. The stillman was in charge then,' he says. But the change is quality-driven, as Jim explains: 'We have made a great effort to get the phenols in; we want to ensure we get the cut exactly right-it's easy to miss. That doesn't mean the personal touch isn't vital. We rely on people in this industry.'

Older distillers' techno-fears aren't so much a Luddite response as a worry that the character of their whisky may change. The people at Highland Park regard theirs not as a product but as a part of themselves. They feel it and nurture it from the barley to the bottle. That's a skill no machine can replicate, a skill that has given the world this perfect synthesis of honeyed fruit, fragrant peat smoke and heather.

ABOVE *Jimmy Shearer has been turning the malt at Highland Park for 30 years; one link in a human chain.*

TASTING NOTES

Highland Park 12-year-old

A gorgeous, honeyed combination of heather root, sweet spices, fruit peel/marmalade and a drift of peat smoke. A seductive dram that mixes butter tablet, dried herbs and heather-honey, all bound together by that wispy peat smoke. ✳✳✳✳(✳)

Highland Park 18-year-old 43%ABV

Soft, with dried fruit, butter tablet and sherry. Silky-smooth, rich and complex. Slightly sweeter than the 12-year-old, with some chocolate, heather, polished wood and Moorish spices. Complex and rewarding. ✳✳✳✳✳

PULTENEY

It takes some effort to get to Wick, and Scotland's most northerly mainland distillery. The railway snakes along the coast, through fertile valleys (or straths), past windswept golf courses, cutting through the wild, bleak country to the sea. Out on a limb certainly … but Wick wasn't always like this.

Until the early 20th century Wick was one of Europe's largest herring ports; a town filled to bursting with a wildly volatile mix of Scots, English, Germans, Scandinavians and Russians. With thirsty people to satisfy, the distillery became a social necessity.

Talking to assistant manager Malcolm Waring, it becomes apparent that everything is that wee bit different at Pulteney. For example, they use a four-, rather than three-water system in the mash tun, which is squeezed into a tiny room. There's one washback in the stillhouse, a relic of an intended expansion that never materialized. The ferments are long by industry standards and air is blown through the wash every few hours to keep the yeast in suspension. 'If you are down at 40 hours you'll be distilling water and sugar,' argues Malcolm. 'You'll get extra flavours, but are they the right ones? For me, you need extra hours of ferment for extra flavour.'

Nothing can prepare you for the extraordinary still house. The first thing to

LEFT *The weirdest wash still in Scotland. The owner lopped its neck off as it was too tall for the stillhouse.*

most of its production ended up in blends until 1995, when the distillery was sold to those canny people at Inver House. 'It's the best thing that's happened to this place,' says Malcolm. 'You felt you were just a statistic to our old owners. Now the feeling is more like a family. I get the feeling that the accountants and scientists will only be happy when they get one big distillery making everything. We've still got craftsmanship and individuality here.'

With a better wood policy and two excellent single malts on the market, Pulteney is, finally, a rising star; and it's had a remarkable effect. 'Having a malt on sale does a lot for a distillery,' says Malcolm. 'We've always taken pride in what we do. We're not making better spirit, but there is a different feel about the place. A lot of people now know about Wick and the boys are proud that their whisky is on sale. There were people in Wick who didn't even realize there was a distillery here! Now they're sending bottles abroad to their friends and family, saying: "look what our town makes". You're not just an ambassador for your brand, you're an ambassador for the town as well. It's all connected.'

confront you is a wash still with the biggest boil bulb you've ever seen. If that wasn't disconcerting enough, its neck has been lopped off. 'Aye, he couldn't fit it in,' says Malcolm. 'But this is what gives Pulteney its uniqueness. It can be a bugger to work because the neck is so short, but we take it slow – and that helps as well.' The spirit still is equally bizarre. The lie pipe snakes and loops before passing through a purifier and finally into a worm tub on the outside wall. 'I always think that you force things more with a condenser,' says Malcolm, looking at the tubs. 'This way just seems more gentle.' All of this undoubtedly helps to give Pulteney its oily texture and rich flavour.

This strange gem was little known until recently. Neil Gunn (a native of Wick) praised it in his *Whisky and Scotland* but

BELOW *Before World War I, Wick was one of Europe's largest herring ports. The boats have gone, but Pulteney remains.*

CLYNELISH

In many ways Clynelish encapsulates the history of the old Highland distiller. It was built by a major landowner, the Duke of Sutherland, who kicked people off the land – often for making whisky – and forcibly resettled them on the coast. He then made his tenants work in his new distillery and took their barley as part payment for rent.

The distillery not only has the same utilitarian appearance as Caol Ila on Islay, it also shares stylistic similarities. Both face out to sea and both produce mighty malts, but their main function is to provide robust maritime-tinged, medium-peated malts for blends – Johnnie Walker in Clynelish's case, Bell's in Caol Ila's.

Clynelish's story is made more intriguing by the fact there are two distilleries on the same site. The current distillery was built in 1967, when the old site closed, only to be reopened two years later, renamed Brora, and making a heavily-peated style of whisky for blends. It ran until 1983 but, sadly, is now mothballed. Angie Mackay is one of the last people to have worked at both plants. 'When I started in 1966 we were just using the last barley from the old floor maltings,' he recalls. 'Everything was done by hand then.

RIGHT *The spirit of old Clynelish lives on through Angie Mackay's stories.*

You controlled everything.' He looks across at the computer terminal that's replaced the old hand valves on the mash tun. 'You know, I preferred it then. Even though you can see what's happening on the screen, there's more stress now with these machines. In the old days if you opened a valve you knew how far you had turned it, now you have to take the machine's word for it. There's not the same control.'

Manager Kay Fleming puts a different spin on things. 'There's a conflict in some people's perception between tradition and what you need to make consistently good

RIGHT *The original Clynelish distillery, which was renamed Brora when the new one was built. Sadly, it's now silent.*

spirit,' she argues. 'You should take advantage if technology can assist people's jobs, but you'll always need bodies around to see what's happening.' Angie took me down to the deserted Brora plant, walking round its cobbled courtyard, through the echoing malt barns, recounting stories of the wild old days. He smiled and shook his head: 'There might have been angels hovering above, but there were no angels down here!'

Today's industry may be calmer, but Clynelish is no less impressive and it's a malt that deserves greater attention. It has a rich, succulent almost waxy quality that marries well with the peat and seashore aromas. So what's the secret? 'The water,' says Angie. 'The loch it comes from is in the middle of a peat bog, but it's crystal clear. You can row into the middle and see the bottom. It must be good, because you can catch 4lb trout in it!' Kay has a different, but equally mysterious answer. 'That waxiness seems to come from a sludgy build up of deposits in a cast-iron buffer tank. When we cleaned it we took out all the sludge and the waxiness disappeared. Now when we do it, we take the sludge out, clean the tank and put it back in.' Strange, but true.

HIGHLAND
SINGLE MALT
SCOTCH WHISKY

One of the most *northerly* in *Scotland*,

CLYNELISH

distillery, was established in *Brora* by the *Marquess* of *STAFFORD* in 1819. Its building *signalled* the end of illicit *distilling* in the area and provided a ready market for locally grown *barley. Water* is piped from the *CLYNEMILTON burn* to produce this *fruity. & slightly smoky* single *MALT SCOTCH WHISKY* much appreciated by *connoisseurs.*

YEARS 14 OLD

43% vol   Distilled & Bottled in *SCOTLAND.*
CLYNELISH DISTILLERY
Brora, Sutherland. *Scotland.*   70 cl

TASTING NOTES

Clynelish 14-year-old
Perfumed but robust nose, with waxed jackets/honeycomb, seashells, a hint of peat and sea breeze. Sweet Moroccan spices. A wonderful mix of beeswax, sea-spray and mellow, ripe fruit. Superb. * * * *

Brora 21-year-old 56.9%ABV
That beeswax still comes through, but there is more peat smoke/autumn bonfires. A chewy start, then a volley of lightly smoked flavours: sweet spices, oil, heather, lanolin and sea-breeze. * * * *(*)

GLENMORANGIE

Glenmorangie 10-year-old
*The benchmark distillery style: pear drops,
light orange and citrus fruit, light spice and a
crisp note. Delicate but with a good, smooth
and soft body.* * * *

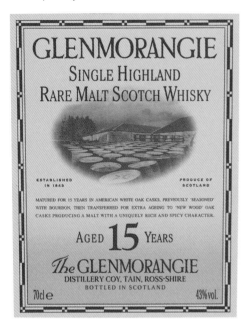

Glenmorangie 15-year-old
finished in new wood 43%ABV
*Crème brûlée, orange peel and vanilla. Light
spice and a hint of sooty wood. A mix of
bracing air and vanilla on the finish.* * * *(*)

Glenmorangie Cellar 13
aged in first-fill casks
*A fragrant nose with apple blossom, fresh
pear, ozone and lemon icing. Soft and long,
with a great mix of blossom-like top notes, a
creamy palate and a salty tang on the end.
Brilliant.* * * * *

Finishes all 43%ABV
Port Wood (* * *) has touches of anise, red
fruit, spices and a long rosehip syrup finish;
Sherry Wood (* * *) has full-on oloroso notes,
tending to nut and spice with some cake mix
and pear; and Madeira Wood (* * * *) is a
fascinating mix of dried mushroom, spice
and charred wood ending with a salty tang.*

Few distilleries have been as transformed by
the malt explosion as Glenmorangie. 'In the
1970s there were two stills and we were
selling five cases of malt a year,' says
manager Graham Eunson. 'Now we've got
eight stills, we're the biggest selling malt in
Scotland and it's still not enough!' There's
little chance that success will breed
complacency here on the northeast coast;
for this is a firm that is forever asking why,
trying out new ideas, trying to grasp the
elusive secret of Scotch. You might expect
space-age control panels, but you won't
find any.

'I've yet to be convinced of the benefits of
computerization in a distillery,' says Graham.
'And I'm yet to be convinced that the capital
expenditure needed to install
computerization justifies laying a man off. If
you replace a mashman with computer
equipment then you have to employ an even
more expensive engineer to solve any
problems.' That was music to the ears of
Brian Gilmour, who was mashing as we
chatted. He was turning valves, nudging the
temperature this way and that, and always
listening; for, as he explained, part of his job
is knowing the significance of each sound –
whether it's the change in pitch of the pumps,
or the switchers girning away. 'The fact it's
manual keeps you involved,' he says. 'It gives
it that personal touch – and there's always
something to be done!'

It means that Glenmorangie's long-
running 16 Men of Tain campaign is no PR
gloss. Neither are these old guys looking
back with rose-tinted glasses. This is a young
team well aware of the needs of today's
industry, but faithful to tradition. 'I'm a
traditionalist, but a realist as well,' says
Graham. 'I don't believe in change for
change's sake and altering production to cut
the workforce is beyond me. Can you
imagine if Glenmorangie was the 16
megabytes of Tain?'

The workforce here understands their
distillery's little quirks – from the use of hard
water to the tall, slim stills that stand like
elegant pillars in the cathedral-like stillhouse.
Their height and narrowness means not only

RIGHT *The Glenmorangie distillery has benefited from the increased popularity of malts, but still remains wary of new techniques.*

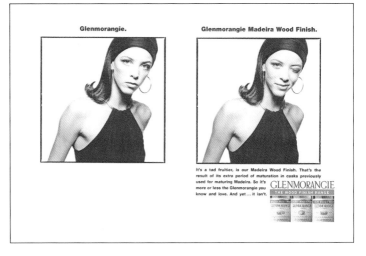

RIGHT *Fresh from finishing school. Glenmorangie puts a different spin on maturing – and advertising.*

that there's considerable interplay between vapour and copper, but that only the lightest vapours can force their way to the top. But running four wash and four spirit stills at the same time takes great skill, especially as some of them behave differently. 'The longest serving man here, Kenny McDonald, has had a running battle with Number Two wash still for years,' says Graham. 'You can come in and he's yelling at it. It just doesn't behave.'

The water and stills each play their part in creating Glenmorangie's spicy, pear-drop and apple character, but it is rounded out and given added complexity by a wood policy, masterminded by Bill Lumsden, that's among the tightest in the industry. Not only does the firm now insist on using only ex-Bourbon casks made from air-dried wood from certain slopes in the Ozarks, but it also controls what type of warehouses are used to age the Glenmorangie stocks. The

10-year-old, for example, has a recipe for first and second fill wood, so certain types of casks are placed in certain types and areas of warehouses. They are pinning it down to the microclimate within each warehouse. With an ever-expanding range of finishes and plans to release a malt made from barley grown on its own farm, the range just keeps growing. Graham believes this is the difference between a malt-led company and a blend-led one. 'I worked for a blend-led firm before this and you were a number. The people who took the decisions on whether you are open or shut didn't know who they were affecting or how their decisions impacted on people and communities. The guys here have strong feelings about Glenmorangie's success. They are the custodians of the distillery and the fact that they make something that's known worldwide gives them enormous pride.'

BALBLAIR

Although the Cromarty and Dornoch Firths have five distilleries (four malt and one grain) on their shores, you'd be excused for thinking that only one, Glenmorangie, is currently open. The reassuringly solid Teaninich, the complex, rich Dalmore and clean, dry Balblair have shunned publicity. Dalmore is strangely under-promoted by JBB and Teaninich is a major provider of fillings for UDV, so it's left to Inver House's Balblair to generate some extra interest for this forgotten corner of the northeast coast.

There has been a Balblair distillery since 1790, although the current site has 'only' been in operation since 1895. The water (which flows through an estate owned by

Harrods boss Mohammed al-Fayed) has remained the same and is one of the 'little idiosyncrasies' which gives Balblair its own special character, according to manager Derek Sinclair. 'We're in Edderton, which means "parish of the peats" in Gaelic,' he says. 'The malt is unpeated, but the water is very dark and peaty and soft; totally different to the hard limestone water used at Glenmorangie.'

Derek also identifies an extra-large, short-necked wash still, earth-floored dunnage warehouses and bracing sea air as the other key elements in Balblair's style. 'It's the little idiosyncrasies that give each whisky its personality,' he says. 'I'm worried that the industry is currently trying to iron them out, because it's these and the human element that make a whisky what it is.' Bought by Inver House at the same time as Pulteney, Balblair has been coaxed out of the shadows. 'It was sold as a single [a 5-year-old] for a short time' says Derek, 'and there was great disappointment here when it was stopped. Now that it is being bottled again the guys have a new pride in their work.'

BELOW *The jewel in the crown of 'The Parish of the Peats.'*

TASTING NOTES

Balblair 16-year-old
Fresh nose, with dried apple, malt, soft fruits and clover. A pleasant mix of sweet vanilla, toffee cream and a crisp, slightly salty, crunchy finish. * * *

Balblair Elements no age
Fresh, biscuity nose with touches of sandalwood. Soft palate, with a smooth vanilla pod/buttery quality. Uncomplicated, but highly drinkable. * * *

Dalmore 12-year-old
A big, bracing aroma, with blackcurrant sweetness behind. A rich start, then complex flavours fizz across the palate: orange, heather, smoke and black fruits. * * *(*)

GLEN ORD

RIGHT *Still life: the steady rhythm of whisky making remains in place at Glen Ord.*

At first glance, the fertile plains of the Black Isle seem a pretty fine site for a distillery: abundant supplies of barley, some peat from the higher ground, pure water. The only surprise is that Glen Ord has always been alone here. Given the fecundity of the area it is perfectly logical that UDV, Glen Ord's owner, has one of its main maltings on the site, making Glen Ord one of only three distilleries to produce all its own malt on site (the others being Tamdhu and Springbank).

Because it's uncommon to look inside a modern commercial maltings, this vitally important element in making malt whisky tends to be glossed over. When you walk into the vast majority of distilleries, the tour starts with the mill and the skill of the people in the maltings is forgotten. Glen Ord, for example, makes the malt for six of UDV's plants, including Talisker, and each of the distilleries needs a slightly different specification of malt-peating level, moisture content, even variety. When you are processing 1,000 tons of barley a week and hitting those tight specifications week in, week out, that's some achievement.

So, is Glen Ord a maltings with a distillery attached, a distillery with a maltings, or a hybrid of the two? For a few years recently it seemed that the distillery had the upper hand. It was to be UDV's trump card, and it deserved to be. Today it seems to have been quietly dropped, but don't tell that to Barbara Ogilvie, Glen Ord's ambassador. Barbara is the latest in a long line of women

to run the distillery – at one time there were five female maltsters working in the floor maltings – and has an irrepressible love of 'her' malt. The visitor's centre is more of a community museum than the usual ersatz showcase and her tales of illicit distilling and knowledge of modern distilling and malting are encyclopaedic. The complete package, just like the distillery.

TASTING NOTES

Glen Ord 12-year-old
Freshly turned earth, sultana and cake mix/malt on the nose. Clean and smooth on the palate, with some clootie dumpling, sugared almond and spice balancing the sherry wood. **(*)

GLEN MORAY

Elgin may be a whisky town, thanks to independent bottler Gordon & MacPhail, but according to Ed Dodson most locals don't even know that the town also has a distillery – Glen Moray. Given that Ed is manager of the latter, you would expect him to be ever so slightly peeved, but he realizes you don't often have to navigate through a housing estate to find a distillery.

Experience counts for a lot in distilling and this is a place with experience in spades: the four men in the stillhouse have 134 years between them, with Dod Grant counting 40 years on his own. Things have changed considerably since Dod arrived. The Saladin maltings have gone, the stills, like virtually all in the industry, converted from coal to steam.

'There were two stillmen here, each working two stills and one side of the stillhouse,' recalls Dod. 'I'd keep the hoppers full of coal, the other, who was the oldest, would watch the boiler. Then he'd go off and I'd have to do everything. It kept you fit!' It probably helped sweat the frequent (legal) drams out of the system. 'We'd have three or four a day-and they were drams in those days,' recalls Dod. 'It was a bit of a fiasco some days, but maybe that's how I stuck it out for so long ...'

He's in two minds as to whether progress has all been for the best. 'When we had the coal fires, this one here [he pats the spirit still] was always difficult to get going. It's still difficult, but it's easier to control.

RIGHT *Whisky for wine lovers. Glen Moray was the first malt to be finished in Chardonnay casks.*

Easy to drink. Dry. Light. Are we talking white wine or single malt, here? Well, both really. Glen Moray is uniquely mellowed in Chardonnay barrels to give a taste that is, to be honest, the most refreshing thing that has happened to whisky in a long time.

www.glenmoray.com

We reckon we made it better in those days though,' and this from a man who has worked with steam longer than he did with coal. 'I wouldn't like any more equipment,' he says. 'It might be more efficient, but it's cold and I wouldna' feel I'm doing the job. This way I'm involved with it and I have a pride in what I'm doing.'

Even though Glenmorangie has owned it since 1920, Glen Moray has been the forgotten part of the empire: when I visited an American tourist was insisting to Ed that Glenmorangie had only just bought the place! Ed is one of the last old school managers and, with 36 years under his belt, he's seen it all. 'One thing that annoys me,' he says, 'is that you get scientists saying that all we older distillers were taught is myth, because there's no scientific proof. Then they prove we were right all along ... but meanwhile we've already had to change everything to please them.

'Take maturation: when I joined, the old guys knew all the best barrels were in dunnage warehouses, but the scientists began putting everything in racks. Now they're going back to putting the best in dunnage again. No-one listened to or believed the people who knew.' You can see his point: if you had an egg would you first ask your grandmother for advice on how to suck it, or ignore her completely? 'In the old days the quality depended on the stillman,' he says. 'There's better control now, but you canna' get exceptional whiskies. That's the price you pay for consistency. There will be good whiskies, don't get me wrong, but there will be fewer peaks.'

Now, finally, Glen Moray is emerging from obscurity. Its light, grassy style has been shown to meld well with finishing in white wine casks, encouraging Glenmorangie to discontinue the old 'non-finished' 12- and 16-year-old and replace them with malts finished in either Chardonnay or Chenin Blanc. It's a bold move, but one that leaves you without a reference point to judge how the finish affects the distillery character. Get your hands on the old stuff, before it disappears.

TASTING NOTES

Glen Moray Chardonnay finish
no age statement
Mix of vanilla slice/milkshake, with spice and green apple. A mix of creamy wood and spicy, estery spirit. Do not dilute. **

Glen Moray 12-year-old Chenin Blanc
An aromatic blend of lemon, vanilla and bran/hay on the nose. Lively, with a spicy, white pepper lift underpinned by soft, lightly-honeyed fruit. **

Glen Moray 16-year-old Chenin Blanc
Grassy notes, with some ripe malty notes and spices. A spicy, appley palate with a lick of golden syrup. **

LONGMORN AND GLEN GRANT

The flat plain of the Laich o'Moray takes you out of Elgin and into the heart of Speyside. It's a gentle landscape and good whisky-making country, but its greatest distilleries – Seagram's Longmorn and UDV's Glen Elgin – are little known.

DISTILLED AND BOTTLED IN SCOTLAND

LONGMORN

Highland Single Malt

SCOTCH WHISKY

This outstanding single malt whisky is produced only at the Longmorn distillery, which stands on the site of an ancient abbey, in the heart of the Scottish Highlands.

MATURED IN OAK CASKS
15 YEARS

70 cl e   45% vol

TASTING NOTES

Longmorn 15-year-old 43% ABV
Hugely rich, mixing orange muscat, butterscotch and firm malty notes. Rich and unctuous: a powerful, muscular malt. ****

Longmorn's dumpy stills produce a wonderfully rich, profoundly complex malt: the mountains on the label are a fair metaphor for the massive flavours of this whisky. But there have been wholescale changes at the distillery: the stills were coal fired until 1995 but have now switched to steam; the wooden washbacks have been replaced with stainless steel; and the water source has been switched. Conventional wisdom proclaims this as dangerous meddling, especially as this is one of the great unsung heroes of malt. Seagram, however, insists that the changes have not affected the new make one iota.

Longmorn shares the same site with Benriach, an important blending malt for Seagram. Another of the firm's single man distilleries, until recently it had perhaps the smallest floor maltings in the business. Every distillery has its little incongruities. At Benriach it's the sight of an attractively-shaped dressing table mirror which allows the operator to see the sight glass on the wash still, lending the stillhouse a charming, if bizarre, feminine touch.

There's another pair of Seagram-owned distilleries in Rothes, this time across the road from each other – the mighty Glen Grant and its little-known sister Caperdonich. The latter was built to increase

RIGHT *Major Grant: hunter, fisher, gardener and whisky-maker* par excellence.

We take a tour around the magnificently-restored gardens, pausing beside a waterfall. Major Grant once installed a safe in the rockface, complete with bottle of whisky, glasses and 'dog' for getting water from the burn. It is still there. We had a dram and talked of when Glen Grant employed over 50 people; we talked of dramming, of the fly-boys and their ingenious ways of stealing whisky, and of the need to preserve old skills in the midst of change. In whisky, you reject the past at your peril.

Glen Grant's capacity, but though it resembles its neighbour it has never made as great a whisky. There again, it was a great place to work if you were a football fan, as the stillhouse overlooks the Rothes football ground. These days it produces an 'Islay' style for Seagram's blends.

Glen Grant is a magnificent example of a late Victorian distillery, designed on a grand scale. It's also where Denis Malcolm, Seagram's former group distilleries director, began his career. Denis is a whisky man through and through: he started as a cooper, then worked his way up through the shifts to brewer and then manager at Glen Grant, then at Glenlivet before finally taking charge of Seagram's Speyside empire.

Like Longmorn, Glen Grant has witnessed dramatic changes in recent years. The soot, the noise, the charged atmosphere of the coal-fired stillhouse has been replaced with the soft susurration of steam, though thankfully the purifiers are still doing their job. Denis may have been instrumental in making the switch and is insistent on the benefits it has brought to spirit consistency and operator expertise, but his heart is still bound in whisky's traditional roots.

'I'm proud of the changes I made,' he says. 'Now you have efficiency and consistency, but if you lose the human element you lose the feel. If you rely on the computer to do the job then you risk turning operators into monitors, not controllers. People aren't machines; we'll always need a blend of people and their skills. If you change and lose your roots then you're like a boat without an anchor.'

TASTING NOTES

Glen Grant no age statement
*Pale colour. Lime peel, lychee and ginger on the nose and palate. Simple, a good mixer. *

Glen Grant 10-year-old
*Pale, with crisp cereal and biscuit aroma. A touch of fennel, lemon and hay lofts. Good, with a crisp, nutty finish, but still very young. Look for the older bottlings from Gordon & Macphail, as this is a malt that needs time. * **

GLENROTHES

Rothes keeps its five distilleries pretty well concealed, almost as if it's slightly embarrassed to be associated with whisky. It's a bit like a parishioner hiding his copy of *Trainspotting* when the minister comes round. These days Glen Grant has broken cover – thanks to its gardens – but you still have to root out the rest. One of the hidden band is Highland Distillers' Glenrothes, which is slowly but surely emerging onto the world stage as a highly-rated single malt.

The manager, Alexander Tweedie, is modest when asked about his charge. 'It's difficult to know quite what makes us different,' he says. 'I can't point to one single thing and say that's the key. We don't do anything particularly out of the ordinary.' Most visitors, however, would take one look at the vast, palatial stillhouse and say: 'That's the difference.'

Glenrothes is Highland's most modern plant, with both mashing and distilling controlled by microprocessors. 'The men don't think they have the same control,' admits Alexander, 'but it gives us consistency.' They also have the final say in the most important elements of production. While the mashing-in temperature is set, the operator controls the flow of the water and the draining. While the flow rate in the stills is automated, it is still down to the men to make the cut though specific gravity meters may not be that far away. But does all this

automation run the risk of demotivating the workforce? 'You have to find other ways of keeping them motivated,' says Alexander. 'They're a good squad and we still need them here. At the end of the day we have to produce the best quality we can.'

Strangely, this high-tech malt is marketed by that most traditional of English wine merchants, Berry Bros & Rudd.

BELOW *The enigmatic Glenrothes hides itself from the public's gaze.*

TASTING NOTES

Glenrothes 1987 43%ABV
A charming, gentle nose with bran/cereal notes, vanilla slice, walnut and sultana. Subtle, sweet and chewy, with some high lemon icing/ginger notes. Very attractive. ✳✳✳(✳)

STRATHISLA

If there was a competition for the prettiest distillery in Scotland, Strathisla would win it hands down. Claiming to be the oldest working distillery in the Highlands, its tiny pagoda roofs, water wheel, cobbled courtyard and timbered stillhouse are charming and the malt is equal to its surroundings – a forgotten Speyside masterpiece. Manager Norman Green attributes Strathisla's success to the water and the reluctance to change anything. 'Monks brewed heather ale on this site in the 11th century and our water source is the same,' he says. 'That must mean something. The size and shape of the stills will also make

flows through our veins, we have a passion for the place.'

This is one of the few distilleries to make the connection between malts and blends: the nosing compares new make with regional malts, grain whisky and Chivas Regal. One reason for Strathisla's low profile as a single malt is because it forms the backbone for Chivas. 'It gives great depth to the blend,' explains Chivas' master blender Colin Scott. 'You can build a lot on it and it can absorb and withstand a lot. Glenlivet is balanced, Longmorn is elegant – both are great to blend with, but Strathisla is the one to blend "on".' And to drink …

LEFT *Colin Scott, Chivas Bros. master blender at work. Strathisla is the foundation stone for the Chivas range.*

a difference, as will the lie pipe that goes up and around the rafters.' He recalls that when the stillhouse roof had to be repaired it was replaced in exactly the same position, just in case the proximity of the copper to the roof made a difference.

Strathisla pioneered the self-guided distillery tour. Visitors can take all day to wander round the plant, talk to the men and relax with a nosing at the end. It's a brilliant idea and a concept which the rest of the industry should seriously consider. 'Distillery tours are no longer places for people to go when it's raining,' says Norman. 'People want to learn more. No-one hurries you here, your question will be answered. Strathisla

TASTING NOTES

Strathisla 12-year-old
Complex nose of lime, nutmeg, muesli and apricot. Rich and mellow with a weighty, substantial palate mixing crisp acidity, dry hay and mellow fruits. ****

SPEYBURN

Nestling prettily into a tight valley on the outskirts of Rothes, Speyburn is another name in the Inver House portfolio. But don't expect it to be at the cutting edge of modern distilling techniques. As manager Graham McWilliams puts it: 'The level of technology here meant we never needed to worry about whether we were Y2K compliant. Things really haven't changed for 30 years here: we still have wooden washbacks, a copper-topped mash tun, worm tubs and dunnage warehouses.'

Graham believes that tradition is part and parcel of whisky's mystique. 'An important aspect of whisky is the way it's marketed as a traditional hand-crafted drink,' he says. 'People's quality expectations are such that

ABOVE *Keeping tradition alive. Speyburn's malt is matured in dunnage warehouses.*

they expect a traditional product and industry. They're buying a complex romantic dream, not a bottle of lemonade.'

Still, it's the desire for quality that dictates the retention of old-style worm tubs. 'I believe the worm allows distillation to be carried out in a slower, more controlled fashion. They tease it out, whereas condensers are more of a flash distillation. Worms are less energy-efficient, but keeping them was a quality-driven decision.' At least now he's over his childhood fear of going near the worms tubs at his home at Glenkinchie, because he thought they were full of earthworms!

Speyburn is making a quiet impression on the market: another malt that's finally earning some attention and another distillery crew receiving due recognition. 'The staff here are what makes Speyburn special,' says Graham. 'We're getting the best yields in the group and that's down to the guys – they've sorted that out. We're not like companies who only pay staff from the neck down. In many ways the men have taken over the roles of brewer and manager. They are not doing menial manual jobs, they have more responsibility and more interest in their work.'

TASTING NOTES

Speyburn 10-year-old

Lightly floral, with a touch of nutty wood and honey. A fruity dram with good weight of ripe apple, roast hazelnut and light clover honey. Charming stuff. * * *

MORTLACH

Mortlach might be the mightiest malt in Speyside, but incredibly it isn't in the frontline of UDV's single malt range. If ever there was a classic malt, this is it.

It's a substantial distillery. The mash tun is massive, the washbacks are solid and wooden, the ferments very long, there's worm tubs and the stillhouse is, well, mind-boggling. Mortlach defies convention: each of its five stills has a different shape and behaves in a completely different fashion, which means that distillation is a highly skilled operation. It's made more complex by the peculiarities of the tiny Number One spirit still.

'I heard about it from John Winton,' says Stewart Duthie, Mortlach's manager. 'He was

spinning at this point. 'Aye, it's complicated,' says Stewart. 'I'm working with a trainee at the moment and we're not even starting on that one yet!

'I don't know if the Wee Witchie story is true,' admits Stewart, 'but it's these old stories that make whisky special. In a year I might be retired and that story could be gone forever.' What's even more startling is that this complicated distillery is run by one man – would that be the case if Mortlach had become a flagship malt? Given UDV's prominent role in industry research, Mortlach will almost certainly remain an astounding malt, but there's an eerie quality to the place, as if its soul had gone. Maybe it's just Wee Witchie at work again.

ABOVE *The old days at Mortlach. Now one man runs the show.*

a notorious chap who had been manager here. He pointed at that wee still and said: "Aye! that's the Wee Witchie. You need to have one run from it in every filling to give Mortlach its true character. It gives Mortlach a 'triple' distillation." Instead of collecting spirit from it on every run, we only take every third run,' says Stewart. 'The weak distillate from the first two runs is combined with a charge from Number One and Number Two wash stills.' My head was

SPEYSIDE
SINGLE MALT
SCOTCH WHISKY

MORTLACH

was the first of seven *distilleries* in *Dufftown*. In the (19th *farm animals* kept in adjoining byres were fed on *barley* left over from processing. Today *water* from springs in the *CONVAL HILLS* is used to produce this delightful *smooth, fruity single MALT SCOTCH WHISKY.*

AGED **16** YEARS

Distilled & Bottled in *SCOTLAND.*
MORTLACH DISTILLERY
Dufftown, Keith, Banffshire, *Scotland.*

43% vol   70 cl

TASTING NOTES

Mortlach 16-year-old 43%ABV
A massive nose: meaty, smoky and leathery, with touches of beeswax, prune and palo cortado sherry. It oozes along the palate, leaving traces of tanned leather, blackberry and damson. Enormous. ****

BALVENIE

Regional categorisation is a vexed issue in whisky: it may be a handy way of grouping distilleries together geographically, but it can be a tricky business identifying a stylistic continuity between all the whiskies in Perthshire or Speyside. But if you can't claim that there is a 'Speyside style', or isolate certain qualities which make Speyside the best whisky-making region on the mainland, how do you explain such a concentration of distilleries in the area – a part of the Highlands which was, in the early days of whisky, a pretty remote part of the world?

David Stewart, William Grant's grandly-titled Malt Master, is happy to admit ignorance on this point. 'All of the quality distilleries are here in this central part of Speyside,' he says. 'That's the mystique of Scotch. We've all got highly-sophisticated equipment, but we can't tell what makes the difference'. He's pretty sure what makes Balvenie such a dramatically different dram to Glenfiddich, even though they share the same site and use the same malt and water.

'The character comes from the still. Glenfiddich is coal fired, Balvenie is gas fired. The shape of the stills is different: Balvenie has bigger stills with shorter necks and that's where the flavours change. Maybe the ten per cent of floor-malted barley helps, but I think it's the stills.'

Other influential factors include great wood management and the use of old dunnage warehouses. 'It's not just age that makes whisky great,' says David. 'It's age and wood.' This underpins his decision to make life interesting (or difficult) for himself by creating a Balvenie range in which each malt shows a subtly different wood influence. 'If we were just to age the Founder's Reserve and do it as a 12-year-old or a 15-year-old, we wouldn't see much difference between them. We had to take a different route, so we produced Double Wood, [where the malt is aged for 10 years in ex-Bourbon barrels and finished in sherry butts]. Then we started doing Single Barrel, and at a higher strength with no chill filtering; then Port Wood and now vintage casks.'

This freedom to experiment is one of the advantages of Grant's family-owned status. 'We can do things quickly. The family is steeped in whisky, but we are encouraged to be innovative, we can go against the trend – with the Balvenie range, or with Black Barrel, where we were determined to make the only single grain whisky that really works.'

If the William Grant portfolio was The Byrds, then Glenfiddich would be Roger McGuinn and Balvenie would be Gene Clark, the underrated genius. David, as Grant's master blender, is in charge of the entire range, from malts to blends to single grain and whisky liqueur, and his special affection for Balvenie is obvious. 'I've been at Grant's for 35 years,' he says. 'It's been my

RIGHT *David Stewart in the malt barns at his beloved Balvenie.*

RIGHT *Pure water flows through granite on its way to Balvenie.*

only job. These days I'm responsible for everything,' he pauses and smiles. 'But Balvenie is my baby.'

What David Stewart has done is craft a range which illuminates different facets of the distillery's character, a quiet, understated selection showing the subtle interplay between spirit and wood. Who said that malts don't resemble the people that make them?

TASTING NOTES

The Balvenie Founder's Reserve 10-year-old
A nose of clover honey, jasmine and cumin. Very soft mixing spice, honey, sandalwood and some raisin. Precocious and one of the best 10-year-olds on the market. * * * *

The Balvenie Double Wood 43%ABV
Sherry notes on the nose, along with dried apricot, honey and burnt orange. Soft and smoky, with touches of date and sweet spices. Superbly balanced. * * * *(*)

The Balvenie Port Wood Finish
Silky, rich and complex; a stunning mix of red jelly fruit, guava, orange peel and honey. Magnificent. * * * * *

GLENFIDDICH

Nothing is straightforward in whisky. Here is a distillery which makes the biggest selling malt in the world, but still uses coal-fired stills, a technique most distillers have abandoned for being too expensive and liable to give variable results. It's a light dram produced from tiny stills, when industry wisdom maintains that small equals big. Only Glenfiddich and Springbank make, mature and bottle on the same site. To be the manager of all of that must be daunting, but Ian Millar is up for it. With 25 years' experience in 10 UD distilleries, Ian knows how to get the most out of a plant.

As a modern distillery manager he has to balance the need for a plant to be cost-effective, while preserving the tradition which uniquely impacts on the distillery's character. 'The lower the cost per litre, the greater the margin,' he says. 'So whisky production is all to do with lowering the cost of the make.' Unromantic? A distillery manager's job has always been about getting the best possible yield from the malt, without impacting on quality or character. Bring three

ABOVE *Snow fair. The first drop of Glenfiddich was distilled on Christmas Day, 1887.*

managers together in the same room and you can bet that within minutes they'll be bragging about how high their yield is. Boys will be boys.

Ian is obviously enjoying the challenge of managing such a high-profile place. 'This is such a diverse site. We have floor malting at Balvenie, we have three distilleries [Kininvie is also on site], one of which is coal-fired, we've a cooperage, we're maturing all the stocks on the one site and bottling it here as well. Working for a smaller company has enabled me to get involved in areas such as wood purchase, which I've been unable to access in the past, so personally there's a new depth to the job.'

As a new boy, it also means that he has to rely on the experience of his staff. 'Working with people is the joy of this job,' he says.

'A lot of the people here have been brought up in the whisky industry. Their fathers, uncles and grandfathers have worked here before them. They've great pride in what they do and are steeped in tradition.' Developing their skills is, he feels, fundamental to making Glenfiddich tick. 'Traditionally, managers and brewers haven't given the operators enough credit for what they have done. The way things are developing it's the operators who are taking more responsibility, whereas in the past they would look up and ask what to do.

'We didn't give them an understanding of the process,' he adds. 'If people are more involved and have more responsibility they're more likely to monitor the quality of the spirit. If they're not involved, it's down to you.'

Glenfiddich is up there to be shot at, but no matter what the rest of the trade or the critics say, it keeps on selling. Its site may be a tourist trap (but then it does give free tours), and it may be seen as a sign of weakness or innocence to say you like a dram of 'Fiddich, but can millions of consumers be that wrong? OK, it's not the greatest malt in Scotland, but it has never claimed to be. In its standard issue it's a perfectly decent (and mixable) drink – a Strauss waltz rather than a Mahler symphony. The newest expressions, the likes of Solera, Millennium and 25-year-old, point to a degree of substance behind the froth.

TASTING NOTES

Glenfiddich Special Reserve
Hay-like and grassy, with some pear. A sweet start, with a touch of peanut brittle on the finish. *

Glenfiddich 12-year-old
A malty/oatcake nose with some grassiness. Sweet in the mouth with a mix of white chocolate and gorse. A spicy, creamy little number with a tingling finish. ***(*)

Glenfiddich 15-year-old Solera Reserve
A mix of dried fruits and milk chocolate on the nose. Touch of fruit and some walnut/orange sherry notes. Crisp, with a finish of fresh raspberries, chocolate and cream. **

Glenfiddich Ancient Reserve 18-year-old
A waft of cereal/bran notes and some sherry wood. A little peat smoke and mocha. The finish has a hint of caramel. ***

Glenfiddich Millennium Reserve 21-year-old
Lovely nose of fresh flowers, nuts and ripe red plums. Soft and quite chocolatey to start; velvety, with a mix of vanilla pod and coffee bean on the very long finish. Subtly charming. ***(*)

THE MACALLAN

Every distillery has its little quirks, but few have such an array of idiosyncrasies as this distillery, perched on a hill overlooking the Spey. It has always been eccentric. Ex-bosses Hugh Mitcalfe, Willie Phillips and Frank Newlands were obsessed with quality, independence and doing things their way. Sadly, all are gone – a great loss to the industry – but The Macallan is now in the hands of David Robertson, one of the brightest new distillers on the scene.

But is The Macallan's insistence on specific barley type, wood type, yeast mix and distillation practise wilfully perverse? 'I wouldn't say so,' says David, giving me a strange look and ticking off each of the articles of faith that set The Macallan apart. 'I doubt if two distilleries [the other being Glengoyne] would insist on using

Golden Promise barley just for the hell of it. We've tested other strains and we lost the guts and oiliness in the spirit. As far as yeast goes, we think the mix of different strains adds complexity.'

You only need to look at the stillhouse to realize that something very different is going on here. Tiny hunch-backed stills are crammed together, fires roaring beneath them, rummagers grinding away. 'These are the smallest direct-fired spirit stills in the industry,' says David. 'The direct firing makes a difference: the rummager freshens up and exposes the copper and helps produce the fruity, fragrant, oily character of the new make.'

It takes a special skill to operate them. 'You have to be pre-emptive,' explains David. 'Direct firing means it takes longer to cool

ABOVE *Pretty as a picture, but some quirky things go on behind Macallan's elegant exterior.*

than steam, so you have to judge what's going to happen.' Given that small stills need to be run slowly and The Macallan insists on a minuscule middle cut, the stillmen here are true artists. 'I know that each man has his own foibles and you could argue that he should and could do the same every eight hours, but part of the fun of The Macallan is that everyone has their own way of doing things. I'd like to think that it's people that make the difference in distilling – regimenting the process will make a difference.'

Since taking over, David has had his nose in every cask, trying to unravel the secret beauty of ex-sherry butts made of Spanish oak. 'For many years wood management was merely checking to see if a cask leaked or not. We've been guilty of stipulating "sherry wood" without knowing why. I want to raise the level of debate.' A nosing with David underlines his belief that it isn't the sherry that makes The Macallan, but the wood itself. 'Sherry actually has very little influence on the spirit; it's a cleansing agent for the cask. What we're seeing in The Macallan isn't the wine, but the wood character – the resinous, spicy, clove-like aromas of Spanish oak.'

His argument is that by using these casks The Macallan adds extra layers of flavour to an already rich and complex new make.

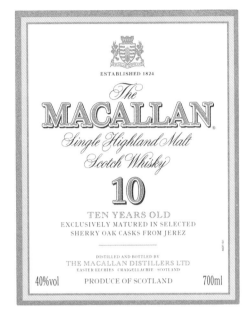

Sherry may matter in finishes (particularly if you use American oak), but not in extended maturation. Well, that's the theory …

He laughs. 'We'll never get to the bottom of it. The more stones you lift, the more you uncover and the more you have to dig again. I'd like to discover everything, but the day is coming when we'll know how to produce a hundred different new makes on one site. When it does, it will give places like this the chance to blow our trumpet even harder.'

TASTING NOTES

The Macallan 12-year-old
A savoury mix of fresh coffee, incense, autumn bonfires and Seville oranges. The palate has barbecue wood, smoke, dried fruit and nuts and lemon marmalade. A cracking youngster. ✳✳✳✳

The Macallan 18-year-old distilled 1979
Amber colour, with richly aromatic nose of heather blossom, chestnut, orange, pine resin and allspice. Slightly oily on the palate. Fragrant but muscular – like a drag queen. ✳✳✳✳✳

The Macallan Gran Reserva
Liquorice, prune and lapsang suchong on the nose, along with a strange lift of pink grapefruit and clove. Huge, but the wood is a little too dominant. ✳✳✳

The Macallan 30-year-old
Ripe and powerful, with orange and ginger marmalade, smoke, allspice, clove and bergamot. Filled with mellow autumnal fruitfulness. ✳✳✳✳(✳)

ABERLOUR

When I first met Aberlour's Alan Winchester he was playing The Macallan's David Robertson at snooker. The industry is like this: marketing departments may hate each other, but managers socialize and share tips. They might talk up their own malts, but there's mutual respect – and a lot of friendly abuse.

A visit to Alan will take you not just round Aberlour, but into the workings of Speyside. It's a snapshot of the history of the old distillers, the unique appeal of an area he loves. He'll engage you with stories of the old owners, of the wild men, of how during the war men would steal the wash from Aberlour and distil their own hooch under the falls. 'I've always said the reason the distillery is here is down to its magical location,' he says. 'This is the only distillery in the village. Rothes has five, Dufftown seven, but we have only Aberlour. There must be something special about this place.

'The water must have made a difference, as well,' admits Alan. 'Current research suggests that it isn't as important as we thought, but if water wasn't an issue we might as well have mashed out of the Spey and not worried about springs drying up. It must make a difference. The old guys would have experimented; found a site, distilled there and if they didn't like it, shifted to somewhere else.'

This is Alan's logical reason for why Speyside sprang, fully formed, from the mess of illegal distilling to lead the infant Scotch industry. 'It's secluded. You had everything here. This distillery is shoehorned into the valley and would have been the site of illegal distilling back in the 19th century. You can go way back into the hill from here and never be found, the haughs over there next to the Spey grew early barley. Then Glenlivet started up, the blenders liked the style and the railway came. There again, maybe they were just born distillers here – they had plenty of practise!'

He's a laid-back raconteur who will praise other people and their whiskies in order to illustrate his point about Aberlour. This is an industry that's interlinked. 'If you speak to me of a distillery I think of the people who work there,' he says. 'If you say "Bowmore"

I think of Jim McEwan, not the whisky.'

Speyside's fame seemed to have bypassed Aberlour until recently, although it was one of the first distilleries to bottle its malt. These days, owner Pernod-Ricard seems intent on making up for lost time and it feels like a new expression is released every week. It's good news for the consumer, because Aberlour is showing the fruit (literally) of the improvement in its wood policy and specifically the increase in the amount of Spanish oak sherry butts.

But, as Alan is quick to point out, there is more than one way to make whisky. 'What suits Aberlour might not work somewhere else: everything depends on the type of spirit you're trying to produce. Glenfarclas thought stopping direct firing took the guts away from their spirit, but Aberlour seems to have improved since that happened. That's the beauty of this industry; there are so many different ideas.' For a manager in a relatively stressful occupation he seems remarkably relaxed. He grins. 'That's another Speyside character. You should see the turmoil inside!'

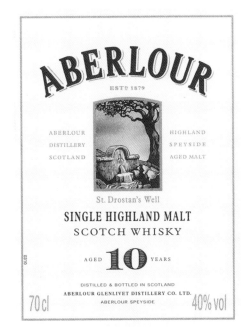

TASTING NOTES

Aberlour 10-year-old 43%ABV
Burnt toffee/treacle on the nose. Sweet as toffee. ***

Aberlour 15-year-old 43%ABV
Light nuttiness with currant leaf, flowers, raisin and mint. Clean, with a mix of cedar wood and creamy toffee on the finish. Very good. ****(*)

Aberlour 18-year-old sherry matured 43%ABV
Fruit and nuts, with a hint of tablet and peat smoke. A sweet start, but increasingly savoury and tannic in the mouth, with hints of chestnut and walnut. ***(*)

Aberlour a'bunadh no age statement 59.6%ABV
Fragrant mix of bonfires, mint leaf, burnt orange peel and a coffee/toffee finish. A beauty. ****

LEFT *A worthy band. 'If you speak to me about a distillery, I think of its people,' says today's manager Alan Winchester.*

CARDHU

Distilling has a habit of getting under your skin. Whether it's the smell of the malt, the aromas of the washbacks or the humming energy of the stillhouse, it's an intoxicating trade in every sense. Once you are in, you're in for life. Given that whisky making is a rural occupation and that large distilleries used to be more like villages than plants, there's little surprise that the skills tend to be passed down through the generations. There are plenty of great distilling families in Scotland, but few as remarkable as that of Peter Warren, currently manager at Cardhu.

All Peter's family is involved in whisky. His father was manager at Glenturret and Ben Nevis, one of his uncles managed Lochside, another was at Edradour. Peter started in a brewery maltings in Dundee, before moving with his father to make whisky in India. On his return to Scotland Peter became brewer at Knockando, then manager at Glen Spey, then Auchroisk before becoming group manager for J&B's four

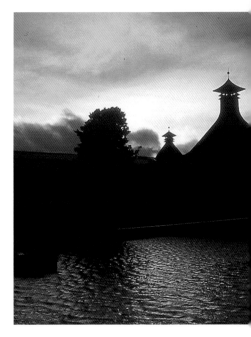

Speyside distilleries. After the UD/IDV merger he took over responsibility for Cragganmore, Knockando, Glen Spey and, significantly, Cardhu. 'Significantly', because this was where his grandfather had worked at the turn of the century and Cardhu's water comes from the old Warren family farm. A whisky circle has been completed.

'I hadn't seen a photo of my grandfather, until I came here – and there he was, hanging on the wall,' says Peter, looking at a faded print of a fearsomely bearded Victorian worker. 'And that's my uncle,' he points to a shot from the 1920s. 'And that wee boy on his knee was my first manager at Glen Spey. I've come back to my roots.'

Quite whether his grandfather would recognize 21st-century whisky making is another question. He worked in a time of hard physical labour, where men were bribed with drams to do the dirtiest jobs. Peter, it transpires, was the man in charge when the drams were stopped. 'We were encouraging people to drink,' he says. 'How could you blame a man for making a mistake by being drunk, if you gave them the drink!'

Cardhu is now a showpiece distillery and the official home to Johnnie Walker. Computer consoles have replaced valves, but

TASTING NOTES

Cardhu 12-year-old
Light and faintly meadow-like, with a hint of lemon peel. Sweet-tasting with a lick of cream, but pretty short. **

LEFT *Cardhu's pagodas silhouetted against the Speyside gloaming.*

operators. How many times do people put equipment in and it doesn't work, because they haven't asked the staff? They are our greatest asset.'

Not that innovation would surprise Cardhu's founder, Elizabeth Cumming. She closed the original Cardow, built the current plant, sold the old stills to Glenfiddich and installed new ones. The new whisky so impressed Alec Walker that he bought the distillery and placed the malt at the core of the Johnnie Walker blends.

Peter is typical of the new-style distillery manager – the public face of the malt and a bridge between marketing and production, a subtle change from the past. 'In my father's day, the doctor, the minister and the distillery manager were the three pillars of the community, and the managers were like gods. One of my jobs is to be part of the local community. The difference from the old days is that now you get involved. We have an important role to play.'

Peter is quick to counter suggestions that this has led to a relegation of skills. 'Instead of the operator turning a valve, he pushes a button, but he still needs to know when to push it,' he says. 'This system gives people a better understanding. Gone are the days when you say mash at 64° and he'd do it. Now they ask why. I've always involved the

BELOW *A family affair. Manager Peter Warren's grandfather (standing second right) worked at Cardhu in the 1870s.*

TAMDHU

Though it's no more than a mile from
Cardhu, you have to keep your eyes peeled to
find Highland Distiller's Tamdhu. The
bottled malt is a secondary brand for
Highland, but it's a core player in Grouse
and Dunhill blends. Good though its dram
is, Tamdhu's main claim to fame is that it is
one of only three distilleries to produce all
its own malt and the only one still using
Saladin boxes.

BELOW *Tamdhu's
giant stills make a malt
which is at the heart of
many great blends.*

There's no doubt that floor malting is more picturesque, but the skill and care evidently taken at Tamdhu is equal to that taken by the men and women who work the floors. The fact that they are producing considerably larger volumes here (40 tons of green malt goes into Tamdhu's kiln every day) does not mean that this is a sloppier approach.

Tamdhu's 10 massive Saladins are huge, room-sized boxes each capable of holding 22 tons of barley. Working in pairs, two of them will fill one kiln. There are fans under the box's mesh floor that blast warm air through the four foot-deep bed of malt, while an Archimedes screw turns the malt, keeping the temperature even. It's a precise operation. Different strains germinate quicker than others, while the ambient temperature will affect the speed of the germination. By regularly monitoring the speed and temperature the maltman can adjust the temperature of the air being blown through and gauge how often the barley needs to be turned.

As Sandy Coutts says: 'One degree of temperature will change the outcome, so it's monitored all the time. Prior to having the computer it was all manual, and to adjust the temperature you had to crank a handle. You couldna' control that as efficiently as you can now.' His pride in his job is just the same as his colleagues' in the distillery itself. 'We make good malt here; they are screaming out for it.' Good enough not just for Tamdhu itself, but Highland Park and Glen Rothes as well.

The maltings are a weird mix of ancient and modern: you could be below deck of a cargo ship, or in the bowels of a space freighter. The latter seemed the more likely as Marion Ferguson took me into the – frankly terrifying- kiln, where huge fans were blasting out hot air and stalactites of damp malt festooned the metal girders. You could imagine Alien lurking in its darkened recesses.

She asks me if I had noticed the change in smell. The boxes outside had a rich, cereal aroma. Here in the kiln there was the roasted, toasty smell of golden malt being dried under our feet. She asked the same question later as we were peering into one of the distillery's wooden washbacks. 'I always smell overripe pears and apples here: the smell is totally different at Glen Rothes.' Once again it's the little things that make the difference. 'Do you see how it's fizzing at the side there?' asks Marion, pointing at a faint, rapid movement in the wash. 'That only happens late in the ferment; it's like a secondary fermentation where the acids are being converted. You have to take that extra time – making whisky isn't like making motor cars, it's about taking your time.'

It's also about attention to detail. The maltman checking for tiny fluctuations in temperature, the stillman adjusting the times of the cuts to compensate for the tiny peculiarities of each of his stills. This might take place out of the public gaze, but that doesn't mean quality takes a back seat.

TASTING NOTES

Tamdhu no age statement
A crisp, straw-like green nose. Crisp yet mellow. *

KNOCKANDO

That hidden road to Tamdhu leads onto another gem of a distillery, Knockando. Like Tamdhu, it's a self-contained little community, with many of the distillery workers and their families still living in the row of houses next to the entrance.

It's also the final piece in a remarkable trio of malts. This tiny corner of Speyside produces malts which lie at the core of three of the greatest blends – Cardhu for Johnnie Walker, Tamdhu for Famous Grouse and Knockando for J&B. Three malts, but three very different characters. 'We draw different waters,' explains Innes Shaw, Knockando's charming, quietly-spoken manager. 'But the real difference is the shape of the stills, the distillation technique – like the length of the head, the speed, the temperature – and wood policy.

'Here we're very lightly-peated, we prefer to use spring barley, we fill predominantly into ex-Bourbon casks and we cut quite early as well. That means we're getting a lot of the esters that come across at the beginning of the run. You get these lovely light aromas, then that sweetness falls away into cereal,' Innes bubbles away. 'We cut before it becomes mealy and then goes oily and feinty. The dominant feature of Knockando is sweetness. It gives us high energy costs, but it's done for quality reasons.'

It's a spotless place; the thick stone walls of the dunnage warehouses sparkle in the sun, and for Innes their dark, damp, cool interiors are another clue to Knockando's secrets. 'It's traditional, I think, but it also helps mature the whisky nice and slow. Most of the barrels are Bourbon hogsheads as well; I prefer that.' I ask him why, expecting a long lecture. 'Barrels are awfu' small,' he replies. 'You have to bend awfu' far to push them!' He recounts tales of how the old warehousemen always knew where the best warehouse was – and

TASTING NOTES

Knockando 1986 bottled 1998

A mix of grass, meal and apple blossom on the nose. Slightly acidic on the palate. Very drinkable. **

where inside lay the best cask – and of the tricks and pranks they got up to, trying to evade the resident excise officer.

Even though they would get an official dram, the guys couldn't resist trying to outfox authority. Innes recalls the day the drams stopped, reeling off the date as if it was written on a tombstone. 'On that day I had one man who phoned in and said he was never coming back … and he never did.'

Today's sober industry may have fewer 'characters', but Innes believes the situation has improved dramatically. 'Everyone's

taking more responsibility and greater pride in their work.' He was backed up, unprompted, by two of his operators, Andrew Grant and Richard Coutts. Automation in mashing has been good news, as far as Andrew is concerned. 'I'm in control – it also saves running around always opening valves. It doesn't mean I'm against tradition; you have to find a happy medium.' Richard chips in: 'They never told you anything in the past, you just got orders. It's much better knowing why you're doing something; you understand it better.'

Today's industry is all about striking that tricky balance between modernisation and tradition. 'You live and work with the same people,' says Innes, looking up at the row of houses with children playing in their gardens. 'Nowadays no-one would build distillery houses like that. It dates back to the beginning of whisky. It is a people product: you need people to drink it and people to make it, but sometimes people only do what the shareholders want.'

GLENFARCLAS

The contrast between Knockando and Glenfarclas couldn't be greater. The former is owned by a multinational and makes a delicate, almost fragile dram; the latter is one of the last family-owned independents and makes one of the richest and most voluptuous malts – not just in Speyside, but in Scotland. Taking its water from the slopes of the Speyside sentinel, Ben Rinnes, Glenfarclas is another example of the crofter-distiller turning his back on moonshining post-1823 and going legit.

In 1836, a licence was given to the tenant of Rechlerich farm, but Glenfarclas' story really began to unfold when John Grant bought the distillery in 1865. These days, his great-great grandson, also called John, runs the operation. Not many distillers can say that their family has been making whisky independently and on the same site for five generations. In an industry where consolidation and stock-market listings have become the norm, the Grants remain proudly and defiantly masters of their own destiny.

The fact that their whisky is rightly regarded as one of Speyside's great drams undoubtedly helps and, for John Grant, the secret of Glenfarclas first appears in the stillhouse. Although here they believe that size matters – no other distillery in Speyside has such large stills – the way they are heated is of greater importance. 'We've kept direct firing,' says John, 'which I believe gives us a superior quality whisky. I'm speaking from experience, as we put in steam coils in 1981 and ran a trial for one week. It took the body and guts out of the whisky.' Intriguingly, the only other two direct-fired stills in Speyside are at The Macallan and Glenfiddich, both of which are privately-owned. Make of that what you will.

What is certain is that direct firing, the rummagers exposing the copper and the reflux-inducing shape and size of the still combine to give a new make spirit with bags of character, which can meld with the second of John's 'secret ingredients' – sherry wood. 'We spend a fortune on good sherry butts every year,' he says, 'though I don't want us to be 100 per cent sherry, as that overpowers the whisky.' He remains diplomatically distanced from the debate over whether butts from American or Spanish oak make a difference. 'American oak is easier to play

RIGHT *A distillery wasn't just a place of work, it was a community as well.*

hedonistic richness of the older brands. And it's another advantage of independence. 'Being private doesn't affect the way we make whisky,' says John, in the throes of packing his case for yet another trip to convert whisky-lovers to the Glenfarclas gospel. 'But it does affect the way we run the business. We're not at the beck and call of money people in London, which means we can work and plan 24 years ahead, not 24 hours.'

with: it isn't as knotty as Spanish oak and some people have argued that Spanish oak is greasier, although we haven't done any experiments. I don't employ a chemist as he would baffle us with science; nor do I employ an accountant, as he'd baffle us with figures!'

You don't need a chemist to appreciate how Glenfarclas begins to pick up an ever-richer creamy/chocolate/raisined quality: it simply evolves and the sherry element comes into play.

At the last count there were nine aged bottlings, ranging from the 105 per cent ABV to a 40-year-old Millennium Edition, plus vintage. The scope of the line-up allows you to chart the changes, as the malt moves from the drier 10- and 12-year-old to the

TASTING NOTES

Glenfarclas 105 60%ABV
Juicy, muscatel nose with some butter. The alcohol is a little too obvious, throwing it out of balance. **(*)

Glenfarclas 10-year-old
Pine needles, spicily aromatic. A muscular, rich core but on the drier side of the family. ***

Glenfarclas 15-year-old
Great mix of polished wood, malt loaf, peat smoke and sweet fruit. Powerful, robust and rich. ****

Glenfarclas 30-year-old
Sweet, pruney nose with a touch of rancio – fruit peel, nuts (roasted almond/walnut) and mushroom. Some bitter Seville orange fruit and a powerful, huge finish. ****

CRAGGANMORE

One of the most enduring mysteries surrounding UDV's Classic Malts is why consumers have yet to discover Cragganmore. This is one of the greatest of all malts: mighty, complex and full-flavoured, yet hidden and forgotten in too many bars. The distillery itself is a modest-looking place from the outside, a classic farm distillery with low-slung whitewashed buildings arranged around a central courtyard. Its previous manager, Mike Gunn, epitomized his distillery – a gentle, welcoming, charming man.

Mike is recently retired, but his successor, Stuart Robertson – who cut his teeth at Linkwood and the (greatly underrated) Glen Elgin – has already immersed himself in the peculiarities of his new plant. A tour takes you through the inner workings, not just the surface gloss, and Stuart takes the time to explain the importance of getting the right grind in the mill, which depends not just on the strain of barley, but the nature of the mash tun; and how they sparge on the second and third waters at the same time to get a gentle filtration, but better extract.

Cragganmore operates some of the longest ferment times in the industry: the minimum is 60 hours, but the washbacks that work over the weekend will run for over 90 hours. It's another little rule that contributes to Cragganmore's distinctive character. In common with UDV's plants, the mashing and fermenting can be monitored by computer. 'Mashing's nothing more than getting sugar,' says Stuart, 'but there are so many variables: the speed of the draining, the temperature of

BELOW *The gates are open, but few have yet discovered one of Scotland's greatest malts.*

sophisticated range of flavours enables the whisky to cope with sherry wood (though not too much) and stand its ground when finished in port pipes. A fascinating dram, as a tour round the warehouses with Stuart goes to prove. Yet all this technical talk can make the process seem rather cold. Could it be that under the search for the ultimate truth Stuart is an old romantic, willing to believe that there's still something magical about this spot that makes it such a magnificent dram? 'Of course,' he says. 'Why did they put the distillery here? Maybe they just felt some sort of presence. Maybe that's the magic ingredient … essentially we're all still romantics.'

the water coming in and the wort going into the washback. Then there's the way the rollers are set in the mill, that's where this machine helps the men see exactly what's happening. They used to have mashing competitions, everyone had their own technique, but what you want is consistency.'

That need is equally important in the stillhouse, and only Pulteney and the mighty Mortlach can rival Cragganmore's stills for sheer 'strangeness'. The top of the spirit stills has been lopped off, so instead of the vapours rising across a graceful swan's neck, they ping off the flat top. 'We're making the vapour work harder to get out of the still,' says Stuart. 'Some will fall back and be redistilled, others have to struggle to get up that lie pipe. Because that comes off below the top of the still, only vapours with a certain density will go over. These aren't just stills, they're complex, rich, whisky-making machines.'

Cragganmore's use of worm tubs further enhances an already complex spirit. That

TASTING NOTES

Cragganmore 12-year-old
A complex, aromatic nose of fresh fruit, heather honey, pencil shavings, sweet malt and a hint of smoke. Unfolds across the palate in a flowing fusion of constantly changing flavours. Marvellous. ✱✱✱✱✱

Cragganmore Distillers Edition
Port Wood Finish
Rich, gorgeously ripe autumnal nose with sweet wild fruits (sloe berry, plum), wine gums and rich malty notes. Massively complex palate. ✱✱✱✱(✱)

GLENLIVET

You can only guess what George Smith was thinking when he took out one of the new distilling licences in 1824. It was clear that he envisaged a commercial future for his malt, but whether he would have believed there would be 200,000 visitors to his Glenlivet distillery in the year 2000 is more difficult to imagine. The distillery looks slightly brutal from the outside, but inside the visitor's centre has been transformed into a sleek, modernist experience – a complete contrast to Strathisla, but it's good to see distillers looking forward as well as back.

Before we reached Glenlivet, Denis Malcolm – an ex-manager – had taken me to see John Christie, the parish blacksmith and a former distillery worker. Over a dram in his kitchen he regaled us with stories of the old days, of how he inadvertently killed a horse when it drank a bucket full of stolen hooch. 'I don't reckon it was too much whisky, though,' he added. 'How could it be? I'm still here!' John remembers horse-drawn carts taking barley and coal up from the station, a bustle of activity in the courtyard. These days the bustle comes from coach-loads of tourists.

The quiet calm inside the distillery typifies Glenlivet's high-tech approach to whisky making. The place gleams, a showcase of modernism. Critics would disapprove, but Denis counters the suggestion that this is whisky making by machine. 'The distillation time is the same, the ferment time is the same, the washbacks and stills are the same. The only thing that's changed is the monitoring and the control of the process.

'Having this kit doesn't change the way you make whisky, but it encourages you to enhance the operators' knowledge of the product. He controls the cut himself, the computer is only there to give him information from the remote parts of the distillery, which means he can focus on the

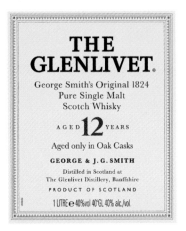

THE
GLENLIVET.

George Smith's Original 1824
Pure Single Malt
Scotch Whisky

AGED **12** YEARS

Aged only in Oak Casks

GEORGE & J.G. SMITH

Distilled in Scotland at
The Glenlivet Distillery, Banffshire

PRODUCT OF SCOTLAND

1 LITRE ℮ 40%vol 40°GL 40% alc./vol.

TASTING NOTES

The Glenlivet 12-year-old
Restrained and light, with some flowers and crisp nuts. Pretty. ** (*)

The Glenlivet Archive 43% ABV
Wonderful nose of wholemeal bread, heather, ginger, butterscotch, dried mushroom and ripe pear/quince. Silky and mellow. *** (*)

The Glenlivet 18-year-old 43% ABV
A classic: aromatic, with hints of demerara sugar, flowers, pear and apple, anise, sandalwood and gentle peat smoke. Long and fruit-filled. A superb, complex dram. * * * *

LEFT *On its way to market – Glenlivet was always ahead of the game.*

most important part of the production. The operator is using the machine to control the process and is increasing his skills.'

There have been subtle changes in every distillery, so would Smith approve? Probably. He was an innovator and besides, the whisky coming across those high-necked stills has retained the classic mix of fresh flowers and white fruit; although, sadly, there's less peat these days.

This part of Speyside has revelled in being remote. If it hadn't been for the absurd laws restricting the production of whisky in small stills then perhaps this great producing area would never have risen to prominence – it was its very remoteness that allowed the illegal farm distillers to make their whisky in an unhurried fashion. Seagram has another distillery in an even more remote part of the glen, Braeval, which was built before Sam Bronfman finally got his hands on Glenlivet. This is the wildest part of Speyside, a place where you wouldn't be surprised to find a few illegal stills nestling in the hills. The fact that this is a one-man operation enhances its lonely splendour, though the garishly-painted pipework inside might persuade you that you've stumbled into a *Teletubbies* set. Today, it's a good, gentle blending dram and rarely seen as a single malt.

BELOW *It may look utilitarian, but Glenlivet is a stylish dram.*

GLEN GARIOCH

LEFT *An Aberdeenshire gem that's looking at an exciting future.*

Despite being one of the most fertile parts of Scotland, Aberdeenshire has very few distilleries. In 1995 it looked likely to have one less when Morrison Bowmore (MBD) mothballed Glen Garioch, in the little town of Oldmeldrum. Much to everyone's surprise they reopened it two years later – in time for its 200th birthday – and gave Fraser Hughes his first managerial job.

Fraser is overseeing a radical shift in Glen Garioch's style. For years, MBD had hammered on the peat, but now the malt is unpeated. A new yeast strain is being used and the cut has been narrowed, resulting in a gorgeously-sweet and fragrant new make. 'Not many people get the chance to be in charge and be in at the start of such a huge transformation,' says Fraser. 'I'm really excited about it. 10 years down the line this will be a winner.'

The superb malt barns could produce three-quarters of the distillery's needs and Fraser is clearly itching to get them going again. Successful trials mean it is a distinct possibility that the smell of kilning malt could once again waft over the village, which has been rejuvenated since the reopening. 'Five of the original staff came back when we reopened, even though they had taken new jobs elsewhere,' he says. 'That shows the faith they have in us. We have to repay that by making good spirit.'

Eleven jobs have been created and, if the malt barns and warehouses reopen, more could appear. It seems to run counter to industry practise. 'I don't believe all that computerisation is whisky making,' says Fraser. 'You need that personal touch. It's hard to explain, but it should never be like a conveyor belt. Nothing beats being hands on; it's graft and sweat that makes whisky.

'I've worked my way up from the floor. Not many people can say that these days and, sadly, not many people will have that chance. I'm lucky and it keeps your feet on the ground.' A manager and a whisky to watch out for.

TASTING NOTES

Glen Garioch 8-year-old
Some turfy/peaty notes, with bonfires and a hint of sherry. Smoky, roasted flavour with a lick of ginger on the finish. * * *

Glen Garioch 15-year-old
Pungent, intense mix of fresh ginger, fabric conditioner and leather car upholstery. * * *

ARDMORE

At one time you could spot a distillery by the smoke belching from its chimney. Now, most of the chimneys have been demolished as distilleries have switched from coal to steam. Fraser Hughes recalls as a child watching Glen Garioch's chimneys being demolished brick-by-brick by a Glaswegian steeplejack. 'He came up the road, bouncing off the walls he'd had so much to drink,' Fraser recalls. 'When the manager said to him: "Surely you're not going up there drunk?" he replied: "Do you think I'd climb that if I was sober?"'

Thankfully, the steeplejack's services have never been required at Ardmore, where the coal fires have been kept burning. It is a massive site, built by Adam Teacher to provide fillings for his blend. 'Teacher got off the train here when he came to visit Colonel Leith-Hay at Leith Hall,' says Ronnie Mennie, Ardmore's brewer. 'He wanted to build a distillery and the Colonel pointed out that there was water and a rail link here.' (One presumes the fact that the Colonel owned huge tracts of prime barley-growing country didn't enter into the equation.)

Ronnie has been at Ardmore for 32 years, on and off. There are fewer men working here now, but this is a reassuringly solid place. Nothing can beat the rumble and thrum of the massive stillhouse. The fires

TASTING NOTES
Ardmore 1981 Gordon & Macphail bottling. Robust nose, with smoke, dried fruit and some cream. The palate is richly layered with smoke, malt and a teasingly spicy finish.* * *
For reasons best known to themselves Allied Domecq has yet to bottle Ardmore as a single malt – though rumours of a policy change persist. Thankfully, the independent bottlers have always managed to get their hands on some.

blaze, the rummagers clatter around. There is a palpable energy, as if whisky has retained some of its alchemical, elemental roots.

Two men work on each shift, each looking after two pairs of wash and spirit stills. 'These guys are the magic secret of Ardmore,' says Ronnie, intensely. 'They have a skill that no-one could ever fully appreciate. You can shut down a steam still in two minutes, but with coal you're always thinking 30 minutes ahead of time. Most other distillers don't have half their skill.' Sadly, Allied has yet to recognize their efforts by bottling their peated, coal-fired whisky as a single malt.

ABOVE LEFT *Like many distilleries, Ardmore was built next to a railway line.*

LEFT *Ardmore is one of the last distilleries to still puff smoke into Scotland's skies.*

ROYAL LOCHNAGAR

Located at the foot of the mountain from which it takes its name, and next door to Balmoral Castle, Royal Lochnagar is as neat and tidy a distillery as you can imagine. But then, you never know when the neighbours are going to pop in for a dram. If the Windsors ever do drop by, they'll be met by manager Mike Nicolson, a man who brings a touch of rock 'n' roll style to the whisky business. A Gitanes-smoking blues aficionado, one of his first jobs when he got to Deeside was to form a new band, having left his previous combo – the appropriately-named 95° Proof – searching for a new musical direction when he left his post at Lagavulin.

A conversation with Mike turns into a mental joust about whisky. It's this philosophical approach to the subject and his communication skills that led him to Royal

BELOW *No risk of the royal family going thirsty when they are on holiday at Balmoral.*

Lochnagar, which doubles up as the centre for UDV's in-company training programme. He's also happy to give a considered answer to the vexed question of technological advances. 'I thought the problem would be keeping the men awake when we first got the computers, and that the older guys would be the most resistant to change,' he says. 'Instead, it was the 50-year-old fellas who took to them first and within weeks they were telling me how to change things. They now have more knowledge than before and can get deeper into the process, so it's more engrossing than the manual approach.'

But is there a danger that the old skills will disappear? 'I don't think so,' he says. 'There is still interaction in the process. We have to be as competitive as possible, but we have to work with real people. There may be a conflict between man and machine, but less men doesn't mean less skill. This is a process that has to be fussed and clucked over and the most important thing is getting the boys working together. I can't do it without them.'

ABOVE *Neat and tidy,*
Royal Lochnagar is
one of the best places
to watch hands-on
whisky making.

Mike believes that the signature rich, fruity distillery character is a result of the long ferment times and the work done by the pair of short, stubby stills with their worm tubs. 'I only make 8,500 litres a week. It's the most expensive whisky in the company and I'm proud of it.' He looks across the cobbled courtyard, where men are rolling barrels into the warehouses: it is a timeless scene. 'All this may hint at a cottage industry, but there is a huge amount of knowledge at work behind the scenes. Of course, whisky making is an art, but these days it is an informed art. It may have looked great in the old days, but what about the quality?'

There is a wider argument. Part of his mission, Mike feels, is to begin demystifying whisky. 'It is important for us to establish the real reasons why each whisky is different,' he says. ' The goblins and fairies may have made effective marketing, but now we're giving you the truth.' Be prepared to be taken to another level.

TASTING NOTES

Royal Lochnagar Selected Reserve 43%ABV
Mahogany in colour. The nose mixes treacle, raisin, chestnut honey with some meat juice/roasting tin notes. Rich, deep flavour – all in all a powerful bugger, ripe and chewy, with layers of Dundee cake/raisin and plenty of sherry notes. ✳ ✳ ✳ ✳

DALWHINNIE

In many ways, Dalwhinnie is what people expect a Scottish distillery to look like. It sits isolated and dwarfed by mighty mountains, the highest distillery in the coldest inhabited settlement in Scotland. Though it was only founded in 1897, this is almost certainly a place where whisky would have been made and drunk for centuries. Dalwhinnie was at the junction of three important cattle droving roads – its name comes from the Gaelic Dail-chuinnidh, 'the plain of meetings' – and in those days where there were people, you can be sure there would be plentiful supplies of the *cratur*.

'Can you imagine it in those days?' muses David Hardy, who oversees production here and at Blair Athol. 'It would have been party time in the oasis in the tundra.' It would also have been a handy place to take shelter in winter. Even today, part of the distillery operator's job includes snow clearing and, until recently, the hostel where many of them stayed kept blankets for motorists who got snowed in on the A9. The weather can be pretty wild for those of us from milder climes, but the locals seem to relish it, talking gleefully about seven-foot snow drifts and of how the old manager often had to crawl from his office to the distillery (not the other way round) because the wind was so strong.

ABOVE *Wild and beautiful. Dalwhinnie is not just Scotland's highest distillery, it's the coldest as well!*

BELOW *Watching the washbacks at Dalwhinnie.*

The more stories we are told, the more new manager Mike Tough looks increasingly worried about his first winter in Dalwhinnie.

The locals *are* the distillery. Every house in the village has at least one person working here. 'They don't just run this place, they look after it,' explains David. 'They are craftsmen, able to do basic mechanical repairs and engineering. We're a long way from the engineering unit.'

The operators have welcomed the switch from manual to computer. 'I'm definitely more involved in things now,' says Murdo Stewart, who started when it was still customary to give men a 'stoorie dram' as a bribe to do the dirty jobs. 'There is less manual work and these things are pretty accurate.' But sometimes the old ways are still the best. When the distillery was refitted the worm tubs were taken out and replaced with condensers. However, the new make changed, so back went the worms – though the old square, cast-iron design was replaced with more aesthetically-pleasing wooden tubs. But the problems persisted and once again the locals' experience provided a solution. 'Worms were new to me,' says Mike. 'I'd only worked with condensers and wondered what two washbacks were doing outside! When we had problems getting the character right, it was the guys who told us

about how the water flowed in the old tubs. We adjusted it and the character came back. These are the only people who remember.

'I've seen times when they would send in an engineer who would claim to have fixed things, even though you knew it wasn't right. But they would never consult us: I've seen a lot of money wasted by management, simply because they refused to discuss things with the men.'

Now the operators are part and parcel of Dalwhinnie's wider marketing. 'At the end of the day, it comes down to people,' says David Hardy. 'They're really chuffed about what they make and the fact that outsiders take the time to find this place.'

TASTING NOTES

Dalwhinnie 15-year-old 43% ABV
Peachy, floral nose with light heather honey. Gentle, but broadens in the mouth – showing honey, malt and a tickle of smoke. Surprising weight for an apparently gentle dram. * * *

Dalwhinnie Distiller's Edition Oloroso finish
Rounded, honeyed nose with cake mix, sultana and a hint of sulphur. Long and sweet with a hint of smoke. The 15-year-old's plumper cousin. * * *

Dalwhinnie 15-year-old Cask Strength 56.1% ABV
Mead-like nose (cooked apple and honey) with heathery notes. A mix of crisp malt ginger and preserved lemon, with a long heather-honey/barley-sugar finish. Excellent. * * * (*)

EDRADOUR

At the beginning of the 19th century it made sense for whisky making to be well-hidden from the public eye. Muddled and often vindictive legislation had made it impossible for the traditional small farmer/distiller to produce whisky and sell it legally. After the law was set straight in 1823 many of the old moonshiners banded together to form legitimate companies, turning their farms into distilleries – the likes of Lagavulin, Glengoyne and Glenturret. But Edradour, Scotland's smallest distillery, is the finest example.

Even from a hundred yards away, there is no sign of this distillery. It is tucked into a tiny glen and when you finally get a glimpse, it looks like a place that time forgot. In fact, it was quite probably forgotten by its former owner, the talented but eccentric blender William Whitely. 'It was only preserved due to lack of investment,' says current manager

ABOVE *Edradour's still so small you think it could fit in your pocket.*

RIGHT *A farm distillery, hidden from sight in a tiny glen.*

TASTING NOTES

Edradour 10-year-old
[Edradour has recenty been relaunched. This is the old expression with the watercolour label.]
A little boiling milk on the nose, which fades to reveal leaf, nut, dried fruit, grass and some cedar wood, and light-tanned leather/oil. A silky texture, with flavours starting on the nutty side and moving to a buttery finish. Attractive. * * *

Edradour 10-year-old
[new style]
Amber/mahogany colour. A nose of coffee cream icing and cream sherry, with a hint of nut and slight oiliness. Sweet and silky. Bigger than the old style, and a bit heavy on the sherry. * *

John Reid. 'Whiteley's approach was what you might call "benign neglect".'

Edradour has somehow survived while bigger and more modern plants have perished. It only makes 90,000 litres a year, in a hands-on, sleeves-rolled-up fashion. 'We're the distillery that technology forgot,' laughs John. 'Thank God.' Everything is crammed into the two floors of a single room. The mash tun holds a meagre one ton of malt and the draff has to be shovelled out by hand. The worts are cooled by passing them through the only Morton refrigerator left in the industry and ferment in wooden washbacks. The stills, complete with purifier, are minuscule – the spirit still has virtually no neck to speak of – and lead to two tiny worm tubs that look more like hip baths. Unusually, the bases of the stills are exposed. This is whisky making laid bare, with nothing disguised. 'It's just one step up from brewing in the kitchen,' says John, but don't be fooled into thinking this is some prettified Disneyland distillery: the three men who work here are deadly serious about making high-quality spirit. The proof is that this old-fashioned distillery is getting the best yield of any in the Campbell Distillers group.

'Whisky making is down to the senses,' argues John. 'You get to know by smell when the spirit still starts to come in, recognize the faint glugging in the wash as it comes in. It is like boiling potatoes.' He is confident that this old way of making whisky maintains consistency in the spirit. 'As long as you have conscientious, interested and experienced staff you'll get consistency. If you're just a guy sitting in a room you could be making any product: here, we're all involved,' he says as one of the men races past, checking the mash tun.

'As an industry we have to watch that traditional values are kept alive. We are in danger of losing our skilled workforce, of turning places into ghost towns and distilleries into sheds, with one guy and a tanker driver who comes to collect the new make. If you get people involved in making whisky, the care, pride and love they have for the spirit, the distillery and the place will shine through.'

GLENTURRET

Today's malt distillery is more than just a place to make whisky; it is often a tourist attraction, an education centre, part of the great Scottish experience. Nowhere is this more in evidence than at Glenturret, which attracts more visitors – over 200,000 per year – than any distillery in Scotland. The spirit of Glenturret doesn't just lurk in its whisky, but in how it acts as a front for the whisky industry. Most people, after all, will only visit one distillery in their lives and the statistics suggest that it will be this one.

The days of 'tour, video, dram, buy a bottle and out' are gone, according to Derek Brown, who oversees tourism for Highland Distillers. 'Distillery visits are changing,' he says. 'The nature of the visit has to broaden to align itself with other things, like food and drink. That brown road sign at the bottom of the road means we're a tourist attraction. People come here for the day.' Under Derek, Glenturret's scope has been expanded to attract not just whisky pilgrims, but

BELOW *These idyllic surroundings attract people for many different reasons.*

conference business, cookery classes, corporate visits and weddings.

Derek doesn't claim that Glenturret is a blueprint for the industry, but holds that there are three fundamentals that any visitor's centre should offer: education, building brands and entertainment. 'The Macallan is different to here, Bunnahabhain is different again; but these three criteria still apply, they might just be in a different order,' he points out. It also means banishing the shortbread, tartan and bagpipes image and looking for something more relevant. 'We're moving from couthy to contemporary. Ultimately we're here to promote Scottish whisky, but we have to give people relevant reasons to come here in the first place. That means we have to broaden the picture and make this a place that can be enjoyed on several levels.'

That means building bridges (literally) with the local community, linking the distillery to local walks and bringing in Scottish visitors in the winter season for food and whisky events. There are three restaurants and a shop, which is more of a whisky supermarket. At the core, thankfully, is the distillery itself which, like Edradour, is

in the classic old farm style. Its tiny size makes it the perfect place for the first-time visitor to better understand the process. The mash tun only holds one ton of grist and the spirit still is the most rudimentary shape in the industry. Visitors can wander around the place all day if they want, asking the men questions.

It may have avoided becoming a whisky theme park, but Glenturret's popularity has ironically prevented it becoming a better-

known brand. Firstly, most of it is bought by visitors, while many 'aficionados' dismiss it as a toytown distillery! This is a shame, because this is a cracking dram made in a hands-on style. As manager Neil Cameron says: 'It's people that make it here, nae a machine. It's all down to their care and attention.'

TASTING NOTES

Glenturret 12-year-old
Mix of grass, green grape and nut on nose. Touch of cereal and apple blossom. Pleasant. ***

Glenturret 15-year-old
The delicately complex nose shows a bouquet of flowers with fresh pear, sandalwood, canvas and nut. Unfolds in the mouth to a long, silky-red fruit finish. A little-known classic. ****(*)

Glenturret 18-year-old
A hint of mint, cream and apple. Rounded, with a mix of flowers, nuts and a little smoke on the finish. ***(*)

GLENGOYNE

For those growing up in Glasgow, the Campsie Fells are a mini-Highlands less than 10 miles from Scotland's biggest city, and a gentle introduction to the serious climbing on offer further north. At their westernmost edge, apparently bolted onto the rest of the range, is a weird little dumpling of a hill – a Sugar Loaf mountain in miniature – called Dumgoyne. And at the foot lies a tiny, whitewashed huddle of buildings that form the Glengoyne distillery.

The buildings give a clue to its origins. Like Edradour, Glenturret, Cragganmore and others, Glengoyne was originally a farm

before an enterprising individual saw the opportunity to make malt whisky legally. But one look at the dark little glen that leads from the back of the distillery, past a waterfall and up the steep slopes of Dumgoyne, makes it pretty clear that this was also a perfect spot to make illegal hooch. When Glengoyne went legitimate in 1833 it was close enough to Glasgow to supply malt to the brokers and, in time, to the early blenders – one of whom, Lang Bros, bought it in the 1870s.

Lang's has long been part of the Edrington Group, which in recent years has become the most powerful independent player on the whisky scene – owning Famous Grouse, Highland Park, Bunnahabhain and The Macallan, among others. Though not immediately apparent in the glass, there are some strange similarities between The Macallan and Glengoyne – primarily in the value placed on that expensive barley, Golden Promise.

'We'll always use a percentage of Golden Promise in the mash,' says manager Sandy Lawtie, 'as it gives added flavour to the whisky. Even though it's not the best strain to mash with, as your yields aren't so good, we feel it gives a certain character.'

Glengoyne is one of the best distilleries for a whisky virgin to visit, not just because it produces a cracking dram, but because of its small scale operation. You can stand by the mashtun and look around the single room, following the trail through the wooden washbacks and into the three small stills. If you crane your neck you can even see the roofs of the dunnage warehouses across the road, which technically are across the Highland Line and in the Lowlands.

A complex mélange of casks rests in the warehouses, with a high proportion of sherry butts made from Spanish oak (another link with The Macallan). Most of this is destined as fillings for Lang's, Grouse and other Edrington blends, but a little is splashed into the older Glengoyne malts. There have even been trials with butts which have held different types of whisky, with new wood and even Scottish oak. It's traditional, but

TOP *The Glengoyne distillery in Dumgoyne. 'It becomes part of your life'.*

ABOVE *Leading by a nose. Glengoyne's gentle, unpeated aroma has won it many friends.*

underpinned by an experimental, forward-thinking drive.

'We're very traditional,' says Sandy. 'I'm not against modern technology – if it is properly used it can give greater consistency – but you can't beat good, old-fashioned experience. People will always be a great ingredient in making whisky.' The mix of tradition and innovation has made this tiny distillery one of the most cleverly marketed malts. It seized the opportunity to promote itself as 'the unpeated malt' and though most other malts are now unpeated, none can

promote themselves as such. Glengoyne was ahead of the pack with vintage bottlings and special releases, such as a malt distilled on Christmas Day. Needless to say, it distilled on Hogmanay 1999!

This is a perfect little place; trying out new things, taking risks and most of all enjoying life. 'This isn't just a job,' says Sandy. 'It gets in the blood. A distillery isn't an eight until five operation: it's twenty-four hours a day, seven days a week. It becomes part of your life.'

OBAN

The town of Oban has many faces: a destination for pensioners' bus trips, a gateway to the Hebrides, a working fishing port, the setting for Alan Warner's novels *Morvern Callar* and *The Sopranos* – frighteningly accurate portrayals of West Coast teenage girlhood – and the site of a classic old distillery with a seriously good dram. The malt also has a multi-faceted personality, adopting elements of the Highlands and melding them into a distinctly coastal character. 'It has the orangey, perfumed, delicate notes of the mainland malts,' says manager Steve Blake, 'but then there's smoke and salt on a long, dry finish. It is unique.'

It's the delicate salt-spray, littoral aspect that makes Oban such an attractive, easy-to-like dram, but where does the saltiness come from? The distillery is by the coast, but very

LEFT *A folly may sit above, but there's no joking about the quality of Oban's malt.*

43% vol   75 cl ℮

little Oban is matured on site. Steve is stumped: 'The location must help,' he suggests. 'The standard answer is maturation, but the answer lies elsewhere; where, I don't know.' Perhaps it's the long ferment; maybe something to do with the worm tubs – which here give a perfumed rather than oily property to the malt. Just another mystery which will, hopefully, remain unfathomable.

Oban survived where other West Coast distilleries faltered thanks to its sea and rail links with the south. Today it is prospering thanks to the Generation X drinkers who have latched onto malt whisky in the USA. That delicate, lightly-salted tang works well in cocktails and appeals to people who may never have tasted malt before. Many of them are making pilgrimages to the distillery, mingling with the day-trippers and visiting whisky virgins. 'It's great to be able to talk to the avid whisky drinkers and to see people trying their first whisky here,' says Steve. Yet another mix, another ingredient in the Oban conundrum.

TASTING NOTES

Oban 14-year-old 43% ABV
As fresh as a sea breeze. Softly smoky, rounded with some attractive dog rose aromas. Clean and fresh. * * *

Oban Distiller's Edition Montilla Fino finish 43% ABV
A fat nose with a hint of ozone and a whiff of lanolin. Mellow and lightly salted. * * *

BEN NEVIS

Fort William's Ben Nevis distillery has had a chequered history. Built by Long John MacDonald in 1825, its malt was an international star in whisky's early days. In more recent decades, though, it fell on hard times and prior to being saved (ironically by Long John Distillers) in the mid-1980s, quality had plummeted. But it was in 1989, with the buyout by Nikka of Japan, that things began to look up.

In manager Colin Ross, Ben Nevis has one of the industry's great characters and distillers. A Long John veteran, he began at The Tormore before restarting Ben Nevis in 1983, then moved to Laphroaig before returning to Ben Nevis in 1989. His 'homecoming' was the act of a brave man, for Colin recalls an event during his Long John days. 'We were doing a public tasting in Fort William and the speaker said the usual line about how there are no bad whiskies. Some wag at the back shouted: "You've never tried f—ing Ben Nevis then!"'

He's evidently a man who relishes a challenge. 'My task was to earn back a recognition for quality,' he says. 'I was proud that we improved both production and quality at Laphroaig, but when it took off as a single malt everyone wanted a piece of the credit. No-one wanted to touch Ben Nevis, but I saw the potential.'

One of Colin's first decisions was to rack old stock into a mix of new sherry butts and new bourbon hogsheads. The success of the 10-year-old and the limited edition 21, 25, and 26-year-olds is evidence of this quality

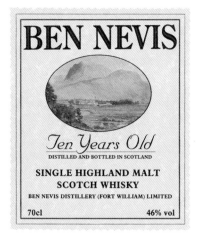

TASTING NOTES

Ben Nevis 10-year-old 46%ABV
Huge vanilla/orange aroma with some smoky/mossy notes. The palate is big and muscular, mixing dried spices, rounded nutty/chocolate notes and vanilla. A powerful beast. ***

strategy. 'We've gone back to basics, started again and can now say we've got something to offer. It is not fully turned round yet, but I'm confident.'

The fact that Ben Nevis is entering an industry dominated by huge firms doesn't worry Colin. 'I'm in a different world to the big guys. I'm in control of everything here. Who is in control at the big firms, where the manager is always in his car between distilleries and one man is running the plant? There's something nice in that the buck stops with me!'

LEFT *A beautiful view of Ben Nevis and Fort William from Trislaig.*

RIGHT *Rolling Ben Nevis into a brighter future.*

TALISKER

Sometimes when you are thanking a long-dead distiller for building his still in such a stunning location, you wonder at the insanity that led him to settle on such a remote spot. Talisker is one of those places: situated high on the northwest coast of Skye, it looks back to the jagged ridge of the Black Cuillin, out into the stormy Atlantic. Even taking into account the reviled Skye road bridge, this isn't an easy place to get to by road, but it was the sea that proved Talisker's saviour, perhaps its raison d'être.

'Everything would have been brought in by sea, by puffer,' says the distillery's new manager Alastair Robertson. 'And everything went out the same way. The sea was critical to its survival – there had to be a sea link to get the place started.' It might explain why Skye, the largest of the Hebrides and a place famed for its thirsty population, has only ever had one distillery; although iron in the rock, the brutality of the Clearances and the subsequent anti-establishment stance of the

Skye people could also have played a part.

Still, Talisker remains a frontline malt for UDV, thanks in part to the tireless enthusiasm of its former manager Mike Copland, and is a major player in Johnnie Walker. The workforce may have shrunk since the days when it malted all its own barley, but it remains a mighty dram. Peaty water, heavily-peated malt and long ferments provide the foundations, but Talisker's secret lies in the still house and, specifically, in the strange wash stills. 'Every distillery, thankfully, has something unique about it,' says Alastair. 'There's nowhere else with

BELOW *Designed by Hugh and Kenneth MacAskill, the stills have a small boil bulb, high necks and a long lye pipe with a U-shaped kink.*

wash stills like these'. The lie pipe has a U-shaped kink, causing some reflux, while the worm tubs add their own little bit of magic. 'The bulk of Talisker's character is created in those two guys,' says Alastair. 'You have to work them slow as well. Too fast and there's less reflux … and less character'.

Later that day I'm sitting in a room talking of whisky, excise men, computers and oysters with operator Kenny Bain. 'It is all about attention to detail really,' he says. 'We're becoming more skilled because we're now distilling and mashing instead of one or the other: multi-skilling, they call it.' He tweaks the temperature on the mashtun. 'They could install a machine to do it all, I'm sure, but I hope that day never comes. It would take away the character.'

You realize that Kenny doesn't need the screen. Making Talisker is second nature to him and like any experienced distiller every noise, every smell has a different meaning. At times like these it becomes impossible to separate the men from the place and the dram. No great surprise, then, that anyone who has been to Talisker (or any other great distillery) can taste the briny air in the glass, somehow feel the landscape unfolding in their head with each sip.

This remains a classic Highland distillery. The majority of the employees have a second job, either tending their own crofts or, in Kenny's case, running the largest oyster farm on Skye. This is a culture where hard work is taken for granted, and so is hard play – as anyone who has survived a Skye *ceilidh* can confirm. Talisker is inextricably bound up in it all.

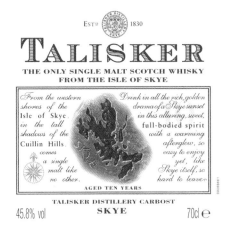

TASTING NOTES

Talisker 10-year-old 45.8%ABV
Powerful, pungent nose filled with peat smoke, charred heather, ozone and rich fruit. It explodes onto the palate, balancing mellow fruit with salty flavours and a tingle of pepper on the finish. * * * *

Talisker Distillers Edition Amoroso finish 45.8%ABV
Good peat smoke nose overlaid with treacle/muscatel notes. There's some heather and chocolate but Talisker's natural rumbustiousness is swaddled up against the cold. Sweet and ripe with glints of fruit cake, heather root and pepper. * * * (*)

Talisker Cask Strength limited edition
Lustrous, almost amber. Complex nose: juicy fruit (dried and overripe) with a touch of tar and leather, even a whiff of iodine. The peat gives a lightly smoky lift. Powerful, with the smoke smouldering around the rich fruit and a long, dry, sooty/savoury finish. * * * * (*)

JURA

You need to make a real effort to get to Jura; first catching a tiny ferry from Islay and then driving through a wild, deserted landscape, avoiding sheep and cows, past the enchanted garden of Jura House and into the island's only settlement, Craighouse.

It takes a special type of person to work here. 'At one time all the barley was brought in by boat, in one ton bags that had to be lugged up from the pier to here,' says Willie Cochrane, Jura's brewer. 'It was kind of hard work. Actually, it was pure murder!'

Jura also confounds your expectations of what an island whisky should be like. The island may be covered by vast tracts of peat bog, but there isn't a whisper of peat in its malt. 'No-one knows what the original style was,' explains Willie. 'The distillery was closed in 1908 and remained silent until 1963. Ever since its reopening its malt has been unpeated.'

When Barnard visited he saw a 'castle-like' distillery equipped with 'appliances of the most modern description.' Little has changed in that respect: technologically

speaking, Jura is well equipped. 'Any distillery has to be financially viable,' reasons Willie. 'That's why you have technology and that's the difference between today and 30 years ago.' For Willie, though, technology is useless without human skill and he has a real love of his workplace. 'Look at that still,' he says, pointing at one of Jura's 17-foot monsters. 'It's so tall only the purest stuff can come over the top. Look at that lovely wee waist it's got. That helps reflux and redirects the heavy vapours right into the heart of the spirit. It's like a waterfall inside there.'

Graham Logan the stillman took up the theme. 'You could make spirit by machine, but you won't get quality. Things change very slightly with every charge and only a man can recognize that. It's lots of wee things, like different smells and sounds that tell you where you are in the process.'

It is remarkable that such an isolated place still has a distillery. Accountants aren't romantic people and when Whyte & Mackay

TASTING NOTES

Isle of Jura 10-year-old
Round and malty. Straw, lemon peel, fresh barley and butter. Sweet, with a prickle of sea air and a touch of peachy fruit. **

Jura's parent firm also owns the mothballed Bruichladdich on Islay. That this wonderful place remains closed is baffling – and a criminal waste of distilling talent. The 12-year-old (***) remains the favourite malt of the Ileach (native of Islay), but the 15-year-old (****) is the one to look for, with its taste of seashells, fresh flowers and delicately succulent fruit.

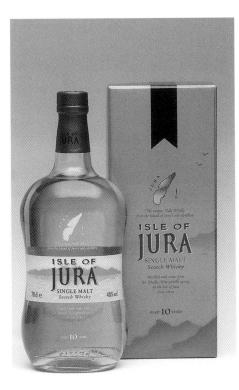

Fettercairn), it made the volume, style and quality of malt that Richard Patterson and his blenders require.

That said, you sense that the guys would like their whisky to be a major player in the single malt market. A distiller as talented as Willie Tait deserved the chance to show his skills with a major malt brand.

Willie Cochrane credits the island's peculiar climate. 'The weather here is different to Islay,' he says, standing next to the two palm trees which frame the distillery. 'Maybe it's the Gulf Stream, but the climate, especially the humidity, is different. If you put a cask in a dark and dismal dunnage warehouse you'll get a great dram. The 10-year-old is better than the old 8-year-old, but if you put it in sherry and leave it for longer … well …' And maybe a wee bit of peat? Willie simply smiles and talks instead of his 23 years on this magical island, of seeing a family of otters on the beach, of summer days when it can resemble the tropics. 'It doesn't suit some people,' he says, 'but I love it.'

bought Jura's former owner Invergordon, it promptly closed down three distilleries. Jura was spared because, under its former manager Willie Tait (who is now at

BUNNAHABHAIN

Islay is a diverse island. Its landscape changes from peat moss to sand dunes, from sheer sea cliffs to pasture. Equally, its malts are a disparate bunch; ranging from the smoky monsters of the southern strip to the moderately-peated Bowmore and the light drams of Bunnahabhain and Bruichladdich, where the smoke drifts in lightly on the sea breeze. Bruichladdich is sadly silent, so the onus is on Bunnahabhain to fly the flag for alternative Islay.

Bunnahabhain's big, long necked stills inevitably contribute to the delicacy of the spirit and Hamish emphasizes the importance of the first distillation – and the start of the cut on the second. 'I think the wash still is more important than the spirit,' he says. 'If you drive it too hard you lose all the phenols and esters forever. Folk seem to think the first distillation isn't important, but it's like an undercoat – without it the gloss won't stick.'

There are few better people than manager Hamish Proctor to do that task. Though a Speyside man by birth, Hamish's residency on the island has made him an honorary Ileach, and well placed to discuss the various aspects of the island's malts. 'Different waters will give you different characters,' he says. 'We use spring water, from the only spring on the island, so you get no phenolics. Then you have the type of malt and different peating levels. We're lower than the rest, but though people say Bunnahabhain is like a Speyside, if you put it alongside Tamdhu you'd soon see the difference!' He pauses, then murmurs: 'I always think of haddock. Bunnahabhain is a fresh haddock, Bowmore is the Finnan haddock that's lightly smoked and Ardbeg and Laphroaig are the Arbroath smokies!' As neat a definition of Islay's malts as any, and typically Hamish.

ABOVE *Bunnahabhain was the last distillery in Scotland to get all its supplies by puffer.*

RIGHT *Like all of Islay's distilleries, Bunnahabhain is situated on the coast.*

Bunnahabhain's light character means it is imperative for the stillman to capture the light esters that come across at the start of the second distillation. As a result, the flow rate has been computerized. 'If you stay on foreshots for too long you'll lose these esters, so that cut is very important,' explains Hamish. 'If you can control the flow rate before you go on spirit you'll capture them. If you're making a heavy, phenolic spirit that first cut isn't as important.'

This doesn't mean Hamish is playing down the importance of the stillman's art, but like many managers he's caught between a belief that consistency is better and a gut feeling that malt is a man-made, variable product. 'I'm old school,' he laughs. 'There may be an argument for more consistency, but this has taken the characters out of the industry, and that's a shame. The more technical you get, the easier it is to copy. Malt whisky has always been sold on tradition and the most important job we have is to preserve the personality of the malt.'

The use of some Spanish oak sherry casks gives Bunnahabhain a lick of sweetness for, as Hamish rightly argues: 'There's no point in taking care making it and then putting it into an old oil drum.' Strangely, it remains a little-

TASTING NOTES

Bunnahabhain 12-year-old
A fresh nose, with light salt/brine. Clean and creamy, with light smoke, some sweet fruitiness and a jab of ginger/marzipan on the finish. * * *

known malt. Peat lovers dismiss it unfairly, while those who have been scared off Islay won't try it because they think it's peaty. But it is the core player in Black Bottle (see p 94) and has a light, salty seaside charm. And there's always a role for a fresh haddock in the shop.

BOWMORE

It was at Bowmore that I first heard someone trot out the mantra: 'It's people who make the whisky.' It was Jim McEwan, at that point Bowmore's manager and now globetrotting brand ambassador for all of Morrison Bowmore's malts. It was also at Bowmore that I had first-hand experience of whisky making, when in a characteristically generous (if foolhardy) act, they agreed to let me loose in the distillery for a week.

Bowmore is one of the last few distilleries to floor malt much of its own barley. Malting is a non-stop process: floors have to be turned regularly, the kiln filled, the peat fires lit and new floors laid. 'Heat is our enemy,' says David McLean, one of Bowmore's young maltmen. 'We have to keep the barley at an even temperature. If it gets too hot the germination gets too quick.' He persuaded me to slip my hand under the surface, which was warm and moist. 'That's why we turn it; to get air into it, to keep the temperature down and stop the rootlets matting.'

After germination the green malt is dried in the kiln for 21 hours – 15 hours over peat and then finished with blasts of hot air. 'You don't want to dry it quickly,' David explains. 'The shell will crisp, but the centre of the grain will remain soft so you can't mill it properly.' These guys don't need gizmos and gadgets; they can check temperature by feel, and readiness by taste. It's about texture, sound, sight, artistry. I try to tell David this and he looks faintly embarrassed. 'Ach, you just get a feel for it,' he says, humbly.

For mashman Alastair Thomson it is about teamwork. 'They say the moment when whisky starts being made is when the hot water hits the grist,' he says. 'For me, it starts with the guys in the barns. If they don't get it

LEFT *Another wee gem is discovered in one of Bowmore's ancient warehouses – some of which are below sea level.*

for 400 years. You'll nip into pubs and trade jokes with old distillers, who will also liven up your afternoon with unprintable stories. Stimulating stuff, that shows just how whisky is shaped and how it touches every part of people's lives on this treasured island.

right, it won't be the same. It's a chain: they pass it to me, I look after it and then pass it on. You need patience to make good whisky.'

Patience is something that Willie McKechnie, a stillman at Bowmore for over 20 years, has in bucketloads. Like any stillman he makes his job look easy: a hundred things to do at once, but done with unruffled calm. You just know that he doesn't need equipment and charts to make the spirit cut just at that split-second when the fierce foreshots give way to sweet, fruity new make; to stop exactly at the point when the delicate smoke stops and greasy oil takes over.

Bowmore is aged in a mix of old dunnage warehouses on the sea wall and some racked warehouses in the town, with all the men preferring the crepuscular, humid, old warehouses on the shore. With a tight wood policy and a mastery of sherry wood, Bowmore is in the premier league of malts. It's a great dram; not just because of the peat, stills, warehouses, wood and the salty air, but because the men have given it something of themselves. None more so than Jim McEwan, whose passion for whisky, for Islay, for people is limitless. In his hands, a tour of Islay will take in 'Stormin' Norman Campbell, Islay's last professional peat cutter, and Arra Fletcher, whose family has lived on the island

TASTING NOTES
12-year-old
A decent introduction, all peat smoke and maritime edges. ****
15-year-old
Is better still, with some ripe sweetness mingling with the light smoke and sea air. *****
17-year-old
This is the one to beat: intense and elegant, it balances peat smoke, Jaffa cakes and fresh malt. A magnificent dram. *****
Cask Strength
Hugely aromatic, with a touch of lavender, toffee butter and fragrant, chocolatey peat smoke. ****
The Darkest
Proves that peat and sherry can work. Tangerine, raisin, ozone and thick cut marmalade on the nose; coffee, clootie dumpling and smoke on the palate. ****

LAPHROAIG

There's little doubt that you've arrived in peat country when you drive into the courtyard at Laphroaig and the kilns are on. Ardbeg may be more heavily peated, Lagavulin more smoky, but if it is an uncompromising belt of pitch, peat oil, tarry ropes and iodine you want, this is the place to come – and that's the way manager Iain Henderson likes it. Iain is another old school graduate, a man with an in-depth knowledge of the industry and who isn't afraid to share

his opinions. This is his kingdom and a tour round his distillery quickly becomes a tour round the industry.

'The reason why whisky is made here is because the water is right,' he says. 'It has no minerals and flows [like Ardbeg and Lagavulin] over peat, picking up some phenolics from the start.' Like Bowmore, Laphroaig has retained its floor maltings, and not for the sake of tourists. 'There's something magic about them,' says Iain. 'If you're an accountant you'd get rid of them, but there are certain phenols which you can only get from maltings.' He stands in the middle of the kiln, the sooty, fragrant reek hanging in the air around him. 'This is our heritage,' he purrs. 'That's what is missing in a lot of distilleries today. It's difficult for a non-whisky man to understand that, but this isn't just a process, it's a living, breathing thing. You can see it happening, see the smoke going through the barley, working its magic.'

Unusually, Laphroaig ages its malt for a month after kilning to get a better yield. 'This isn't an exact science,' admits Iain. 'It's a craft, it's seat-of-the-pants stuff at times. We may be more scientific and know a lot more about ethanol, but ultimately it's the hand of the person that matters – particularly in the maltings and the still house.'

It's impossible to pinpoint what gives Laphroaig its personality, but the floor-malted barley, the peating level, the small stills and the long spirit cut are all key factors. Iain is another believer in the importance of the wash still on spirit character. 'It characterizes the spirit. You create the flavour in the first and clean it up in the second. But there's still an unknown quotient about whisky and this is where it lives,' he gestures towards the seven tiny stills. 'The shape, the size, the angle of the lie pipe all give us that flavour.' As does the wood, which is all ex-Bourbon casks. 'If I want a bottle of sherry, I'll buy one,' states Iain, killing that topic, though the magnificent 30-year-old shows the potential combination of this exceptional dram and exceptional sherry butts.

TASTING NOTES

Laphroaig 10-year-old Cask Strength
57.3%ABV
Ultra-crisp malt fresh from the kiln with layers of tar, lapsang souchong, orange, germoline, and peat fires on the beach. Crashes into the mouth with a mix of bonfires, iodine and crisp malt. Long, smoke-filled finish. Savour and tremble at its power. ＊＊＊＊(＊)

LAPHROAIG®
AGED **15** YEARS
SINGLE *ISLAY* MALT
SCOTCH WHISKY
The most richly flavoured of all Scotch whiskies
ESTD **1815** ESTD
DISTILLED AND BOTTLED IN SCOTLAND BY
D JOHNSTON & CO. (LAPHROAIG). LAPHROAIG DISTILLERY. ISLE OF ISLAY
70cl e   43% vol
L80994

Laphroaig 15-year-old 43%ABV
The peat has dried down, leaving behind a smooth, oily/creamy nose with hint of tar. Sweet and surprisingly mellow to start, with a slow-burning peat smoke flavour building up towards the finish. ＊＊＊

Laphroaig 30-year-old 43%ABV
A complex, nose of dried peel, tar and sweet perfume. It's Laphroaig mellowed into old age – all leather armchairs and peat fires. Starts smoky, then fruit, then the tarry ropes/iodine, all building relentlessly before finishing with a burst of rich smoky fruit. Great balance. ＊＊＊＊(＊)

Iain is approaching retirement, and it will be interesting to see quite how (or if) Allied replaces the man who has become Mr Laphroaig. Old school values are on the way out, as modern management strategies take over the industry and managers become an endangered species. The risk is that by changing the structure there's no incentive for younger men and women on the shop floor to stay. If there is no chance of promotion, what's the point?

In a strange way Iain has become like his whisky: uncompromising, demanding to be taken on his own terms, but with a heart of gold. 'There's a feeling of togetherness in whisky that you don't get in any other industry,' he says. 'And it's the people who make it different. In big companies you become a number; at Laphroaig we're a family, these people rely on us.'

ABOVE RIGHT *The old crew – peat and whisky ran in their veins.*

RIGHT *The mightiest malt of all is born here.*

LAGAVULIN

There's little doubt when you arrive at Lagavulin that you're in the presence of a mighty creature. Crammed between the road and the shores of a tiny bay, Lagavulin isn't so much a distillery as a citadel of malt. Its white walls seem timeless, even mythic: this, you think, is how whisky has always been made. But once inside you're faced with up-to-date technology that may shock purists; but distilling manager Donald Renwick sees no paradox in this juxtaposition of ancient and modern.

'Lagavulin has evolved and changed over the years,' he says. 'But it can't be industrial; it's not in its nature.' Donald is a new arrival at Lagavulin and follows in the footsteps of

TASTING NOTES

Lagavulin 16-year-old 43%ABV

An evocative sea-shore aroma, mixing aromatic smoke with marmalade, nutmeg and heather. Complex, with cocoa powder and ripe Shiraz/blackcurrant pastille fruit on the finish, all smothered in a deep blanket of peat smoke. * * * * *

Lagavulin Distiller's Edition PX finish 43%ABV

Subtly sweet, peaty nose with walnut, tar, treacle. The Lagavulin signature a little muted by the layers of rich sultry, sumptuous fruits. The fragrant smoke finally wraps itself round the tastebuds on the long, lingering finish. * * * *

UDV also owns the massive Caol Ila, whose glass-fronted stillhouse gazes across to Jura. Though peated to the same level as Lagavulin, this is a different beast, more oily than smoky and a must-try. * * *

the idiosyncratic Mike Nicolson, the only blues-playing distillery manager in the land, now at Royal Lochnagar. But Islay does strange things to the psyche, it weaves its peculiar siren magic into your soul and refuses to leave. Donald is already in love with the place. But computers?

'I'm convinced it has "upskilled" the operators,' he says. 'When the guys first saw computers they probably panicked, but after Mike had trained them they were better than him within weeks. It's meant that they can look inside the mash tun or washback and get involved in the bigger picture. Because they have more information, they can make decisions quicker.'

For Donald – and UDV – that helps to keep the distillery character constant. 'We've kept the ferments long to avoid changing the character and it's in here,' he says, pointing to a washback, 'that it starts to take shape.'

The mighty Lagavulin then forms itself during the slow, slow distillation in the long-waisted, teardrop-like stills.

Donald is another manager who is happy to wrap himself in the strange mystery that, thankfully, still enshrouds malt. He doesn't talk of Lagavulin as a brand, but as a living entity and he's right. Every great distillery has a presence that appears to dictate the style of its malt. Islay's weird seaweedy peat, the stills, the slow distillation, the microclimate of the bay and its interplay with the casks in the damp, sea-lashed warehouses all have their own subtle effect on Lagavulin. Men and managers are merely caretakers.

'Lagavulin is about the people, the situation, the way it has evolved,' says Donald. 'It's not designed to make "whisky", it's designed to make Lagavulin! You can see it in the workforce: some of them are working in the same place their grandfathers worked. They inherently believe they belong to Lagavulin, that it's part of them.'

No-one personifies that better than Iain MacArthur, 40 years a warehouseman. An Ileach, crofter, peat cutter and owner of a fine head of cattle, he typifies the passion in whisky people for their place of work. A session in the warehouses with Iain teaches you more about Lagavulin than any shelf of books. He taps the casks, draws out samples of different ages, different woods, and gets you to pour a little on your palms to smell it better, then looks at you slightly askance as you reel off the flavours that erupt. Like many distillery workers he doesn't drink, but that doesn't mean he's short of an opinion. Don't try to praise any other Islay whisky in his presence, for as far as Ian is concerned everywhere else makes dreadful whiskies, 'though I'm not prejudiced!' he adds, with a grin. The spirit of the place indeed.

LEFT *Straight of the peaty hill and into the distillery.*

BELOW *Tucked away in its rocky bay, Lagavulin was built on the site of an illegal still.*

ARDBEG

The renaissance of Ardbeg has been one of
the most welcome events in distilling in
recent years. This, the last of Islay's three
south coast distilleries, had been abandoned
by its previous owners, who considered it
surplus to requirements. With Port Ellen
closed, Bruichladdich mothballed and
Ardbeg seemingly condemned, Islay was
suffering. From a purely commercial
perspective, Ardbeg's closure was perhaps
understandable. But the loss was more than
just the end of a magnificent whisky; it
damaged the fragile local economy.

Thankfully, Glenmorangie stepped in to
rescue Ardbeg, and after a few million
pounds had been spent on rebuilding,
renovating and relaunching, the whisky is
back and the place is alive again, throbbing
with a sense of pride. 'Someone said: "You've
bought a dump"', recalls Bill Lumsden,
Glenmorangie's head of distilleries. 'But we
saw it as a challenge. We were galvanized,
passionate about it right from the start.'
Passion is the right word, though Bill
and manager Stuart Thomson will admit
they're still getting their heads and noses
round Ardbeg's peculiarities. But they are
young, enthusiastic and fired-up about their
new baby.

Deep.

Rather
more so.

Ardbeg Single Malt Whisky from Islay
has a remarkably deep flavour.
Find out more about it at www.ardbeg.com

Ardbeg
The ultimate Islay Malt.

Ardbeg, vintage 1975, is a gold medal winner at the 1999 International Spirits Challenge
Part of Glenmorangie PLC.

It takes a while to winkle out the secrets of
a distillery and its malt. Ardbeg, the most
heavily-peated of all, manages to balance a
complex mix of flavours on top of that
smouldering base. What's different? Not just
the amount of peat used, but the way the
peat is burned in the kiln, the length of time
the fires are lit and the amount of phenolic-
rich husk in the grist.

Then there's the ancient spirit still, which
looms above you in the tiny still house,
adorned with rivets and patterned

ABOVE RIGHT *Ardbeg
is keen to show its
pedigree and its
heritage.*

RIGHT *A fresh coat
of paint and a bright
future for this
magnificent distillery.*

copperwork. 'That still goes a long way to explaining why Ardbeg is so complex,' says Stuart. 'Look at it! It's challenging the heavier alcohols to try and come across right from the start. They'll struggle to get past the waist: the lyne arm points up, so they'll condense and flow back down; then there's a purifier which will capture any that are left and return them back into the body of the still. All of this encourages different flavours and builds a lot of character. It's more phenolic, but it's also more complex.'

A multi-faceted dram it may be, but Stuart knows that if the old employees had not come back to work, his job of understanding Ardbeg would have been much more difficult. 'It's a team effort. The guys have a feel for it because they used to work here. You lose the personality without the people and when you lose personality, the product goes down the pan.' No danger of redundancies here, then. 'The logical conclusion is that distilleries become unmanned plants, which are no more than sheds with taps,' says Bill. 'Redundancies aren't for efficiency, they are down to greed ... for higher shareholder returns.'

This philanthropy extends beyond the distillery's newly-whitewashed walls. Port

Ellen was a ghost town and the café-cum-bar in the old kiln at Ardbeg (run by Stuart's wife Jackie) is still the only place in the south of the island serving a decent bite to eat. But now the distillery has reopened, the local community has come back to life. 'You feel duty bound to do it,' says Stuart. 'We're a money-making industry and distillers have a social and moral responsibility to put something back into the community.' You get the feeling that Ardbeg's best days have yet to come.

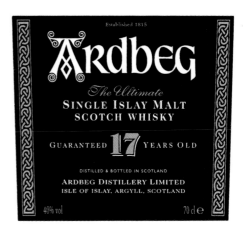

TASTING NOTES

Ardbeg 10-year-old 46%ABV
Astoundingly smoky, yet delicate with a subtle mix of tar, raisin and caramelized apple notes. Robustly flavoured, like someone's lit a peat fire under your nose. A salt-tinged complex finish. It manages to be flavour-packed yet delicate at the same time. ****(*)

Ardbeg 17-year-old
Hugely complex, mixing tangerine, tar, fragrant peat smoke, gingerbread and smoky malt. Silky and smoky, with an astoundingly long finish. Superb balance. ****

Ardbeg 1975
Sweet mix of fruit, heather and smoke on the nose. Big, almost leathery; then the fires are stoked up and smoulder on forever in the mouth. *****

SPRINGBANK

SPRINGBANK

AGED **21** YEARS   AGED **21** YEARS

S

ESTABLISHED 1828

CAMPBELTOWN

Scotch **SINGLE MALT** Whisky

PRODUCT OF SCOTLAND
Distilled by J. & A. MITCHELL & CO. LTD.
Springbank Distillery · Campbeltown · Scotland

70cl   46%vol

TASTING NOTES

Springbank 10-year-old 46%ABV

Full, malty nose with some sea air, spice, pigskin and toffee apple. Very smooth and sweet to start then a fusillade of flavours – dried herb, butter, salt, smoke, vanilla pod, moss and flowers. A great package. ****(*)

Springbank 15-year-old 46%ABV

Well balanced between vanilla, crème brûlée, salty sea air burnt range and smoky wood. A silky mouthful though the wood is a little prominent then a splash of sea spray on the finish. ***(*)

Springbank 21-year-old 46%ABV

Amber colour. Peach, raisin ozone, smoke. Fluxing between caramelized orange and salt. Smooth start, then some heather, raisin, clootie dumpling coconut matting and the signature salty finish. ****

Springbank 1966 Local Barley 54.4%ABV

Huge nose mixing coal bunker, sweetly ripe fruit, hickory wood and almost rancio-like aromas of mushroom, leaf-mould, anise and smoke. Explodes on the palate: biscuity, then some toffee, hickory chips, smoke and sea air. A fascinating mix of sweet and sour. *****

Longrow 10-year-old

Attractive mix of muted/turfy peat smoke with a perfumed rose-petal lift. A drop of water kindles the peat fires but always balanced by a lavender/rose-scented perfume. Silky, briny with a rich coal-tar/perfumed finish. ****

The decline of Campbeltown as a distilling capital came suddenly. Of the 21 distilleries that Barnard visited, only two are still in existence and one of them, Glen Scotia, is open only intermittently. The good news is that you will soon be able to buy five different Campbeltown malts; four from one distillery – the legendary Springbank.

A resolute pillar of tradition, family-owned Springbank is the only malt distillery where the entire process from malting to bottling is carried out on the same site. In fact, flying in the face of convention, the firm reintroduced floor malting in 1992. 'People tell us that our hands-on approach is special,' says Ewan Mitchell, who handles marketing. 'Because it has been in the hands of the same family for so long, our chairman is determined to keep it the way he inherited it. Fortunately we've got a good reputation and consumers want to see it as people-based. Our independence is obviously as important to them as it is to me.'

But is Springbank just an anachronism in today's industry? 'The industry is becoming less and less traditional,' says Ewan, 'but we're against change for change's sake. It's easy to impose new methods but lose sight of the product. At the end of the day we control the bottled product from start to finish.'

For manager Frank McHardy, tradition makes a difference to the quality of the spirit. 'People are totally involved in the product,' he says. 'The guys have to work it, make the malt, mash it and distil it – there's total involvement. We're also employing 25 people in Campbeltown and, given the economy of Kintyre, that's very important.' Frank's tour of duty has seen him manage Bruichladdich on Islay and Bushmills in Northern Ireland, before returning to Springbank; thus he has run three very different distilleries in the 30-mile radius which most historians agree is the cradle of whisky making.

His Bushmills' experience is proving particularly useful in developing Springbank's latest addition, a triple-distilled unpeated malt called Hazelburn, which is due to appear in 2002. It is the third pillar of the Springbank dynasty, joining the

single plant could be seen as simply perverse, but Frank plays it down. 'There's always something going on here to make it a fascinating place to work. When the organic was being made [in 1992, under previous manager John McDougall] the whole plant had to be cleaned to make sure there was no risk of contamination from non-organic materials. It was like making kosher whisky, with the Soil Association as the rabbis.'

Maybe only a small firm would be willing to enter into these kind of ventures: if you only have one or two distilleries you have to try as many different things as you can to challenge the might of the big boys. There again, Springbank has always been individualistic. 'A few years ago we did a bottling called Against the Grain [the creation of Ewan's predecessor, Gordon Wright]. I think that kind of sums us up. We're not in the SWA [Scottish Whisky Association], we do everything on site and geographically we're out on a limb.' Quality-wise, they are at the top.

double-distilled, heavily-peated Longrow and the dazzlingly complex Springbank itself, which is distilled two-and-a-half times, (Springbank has three stills.) There's even an organic whisky.

It would be wrong to think of Longrow and Hazelburn as Springbank with a different tweak: they are three distinct individuals that happen to be produced on the same site. Making three (four, if the organic goes into full production) malts in a

FETTERCAIRN

TASTING NOTES

Old Fettercairn 10-year-old
Golden with a nose of freshly turned earth, hay and crisp notes and a hint of sandshoe. Biscuity palate with some sweet malty notes. Clean. **(*)**

Fettercairn lies in the Howe of the Mearns, the setting for Lewis Grassic Gibbon's classic novel *Sunset Song*. It is a heavy-earthed, fertile plain pressed between the Grampians and the windy coast, a place of big skies, fields of barley and, at one time, plenty of whisky. There was once a clutch of distilleries here-Glenury Royal, North Port, Glen Esk, Lochside. Now only Glencadam and Fettercairn survive, the former in Brechin, the latter just outside the eponymous, neat town with its slightly incongruous road arch commemorating a visit by Queen Victoria. It's a tidy, quiet, white-painted distillery and for manager Willie Tait a change after 25 years on Jura.

Fettercairn is one of those distilleries that you duck and dive through, up and down stairs, finding pieces of equipment hidden around corners. It is a solid, heavily-riveted place with some strange quirks, like the water coolers on the top of the spirit stills and the soap grinder on the side of the wash still. But there's plenty to get involved in, which suits Willie just fine.

'I suppose Jura was a wee bit clinical inside,' he says, standing by the cast-iron mash tun. 'I still believe you should be hands-on in this game. This has more heart; it seems to pulse. The stills are wee individuals, they're so fickle it's amazing, while this,' he points at the mash tun, 'might look old-fashioned, but it does the job and it does it efficiently.'

Like all the best whisky men, Willie isn't short of an opinion. He has no time for what he calls the 'Mickey Mouse stories' of the marketing men: he is grounded in hands-on production, full of respect for the equipment and the skills of the men. 'I've no time for myth, but there is a story to be told,' he says, over a glass. 'We feel that there's something alive here. We don't classify this as a product: the distillery and the dram are like the people inside them.'

LEFT *The big skies of the Mearns sit over its loveliest distillery.*

AUCHENTOSHAN

Outside Speyside and Islay, malt distilleries are pretty well spread out, which puts a bit of a strain on the notion of 'regional' styles. These days the term 'Lowland malt' covers one in Wigtownshire, one outside Edinburgh and Auchentoshan, on the banks of the Clyde. Some region. Still, when you have no neighbours you can get on with your own thing: for Auchentoshan this involves having its washbacks on the outside, pioneering a new dried yeast and, most importantly, producing a triple-distilled malt. It's also a Lowland malt made by Islay men, and that must count for something.

Assistant manager Ronnie Learmond believes the secret of Auchentoshan's delicately elegant style is in the use of the three stills. 'It would be wrong to say we've perfected triple distillation,' he says. 'But we're not doing it the same way as it was done 20 years ago. Now it's better balanced and controlled.'

The change lies in the way in which the low wines are redistilled with the strong feints in the middle still. The spirit is then collected and redistilled in the third still, with only a tiny cut being taken. This means that stillman Andy McColl (the son of an ex-Bowmore manager) has to be on his toes. 'The three stills will be running at the same time, though at different stages,' he says. 'You just have to run them very slowly and always keep your mind on the task in hand.'

Part of the Morrison Bowmore stable, Auchentoshan is now receiving the attention it deserves. The delicacy of the new make means it needs good wood to develop fully.

BELOW *Who would have thought that this scene is only a few miles from Glasgow?*

What is surprising is its ability to cope with ageing in ex-sherry wood – and even a finishing in PX (Pedro Ximenez) casks. It's like Glasgow boxer Benny Lynch: light, but with surprising strength and staying power. But then it's that Glasgow connection which holds it back. 'If only we could take the stigma out of Lowland whisky, ' laments Ronnie. 'The first time people try it they love it, but are amazed something this good can be produced so close to Glasgow.'

TASTING NOTES

Auchentoshan Select
Light and lemony, with lots of sweet bran/cereal notes. Light, sweet and mixable. * *

Auchentoshan 10-year-old
Fuller nose, but bran is still predominant. Lightly perfumed and more solid than the Select. * *(*)

Auchentoshan 21-year-old 43%ABV
Amber. Elegant, with a mix of red plum, tobacco leaf, apple with fresh sweet grass and nut. Almost jammy fruit on palate, with some grass and butterscotch. Silky and long. * * * *(*)

Auchentoshan Three Wood
Rich, slightly pruney nose, with walnut, chicory notes. Sweet, with a mass of flavours: roast nut, coffee, prune and ripe fruit. Sweet and stylish. * * *(*)

GLENKINCHIE

There's a redbrick Victorian solidity about Glenkinchie that seems a little at odds with its location in the midst of tranquil Lothian farmlands. Only 45 minutes from Edinburgh, this is another Lowland gem ignored by many whisky tourists as they head north in search of the 'real' stuff. In fact, Lowland whiskies have always had a tough time of it. Even when whisky was booming at the end of the 19th century there were relatively few distilleries south of Edinburgh – even though logic would suggest that easy access to barley, water and the blending houses would have seen distilleries mushrooming.

'My theory is that in the Lowlands they had always used different grains and produced in high volumes,' says manager Charlie Smith, when asked about this anomaly. 'When the [continuous] Coffey stills appeared, they switched to those, whereas Highland whiskies were known for their different character.' This tradition could explain Glenkinchie's massive wash still, easily the biggest in Scotland, and a key element in producing its meadow-sweet, grassy dram.

It remains a village distillery – and the only one with its own bowling green-though the cattle which used to live on the site when assistant manager Jim Casey father arrived with his family in the 1960s have long gone. The ties with the community and the

ABOVE Glenkinchie was built on a grand scale but has always made a gentle Lowland dram.

environment remain strong: all the men live in the village, the distillery processes the community's waste, sprays the rich pot ale onto one of its own fields and supplies draff to the local farmers. For Charlie it's a matter of common sense. 'We need good-quality products to make whisky and if we don't recycle we're not keeping our part of the environmental bargain,' he reasons. 'It's a matter of balance.'

This is a recurring phrase in any conversation with Charlie, who moved to Glenkinchie after spells at Pittyvaich and Cardhu, though it's his engineering background which surfaces as he takes you through the intricate model of the distillery in the visitor's centre. 'Here's technology!' he says, pointing to a turner in the kiln. 'These people weren't afraid of innovation and we shouldn't be either.' Once again, though, it comes down to balance.

'Here, certain sequences have been automated, but it's all under the control of an operator,' he says. 'They're learning new techniques and are no longer regarded as semi-skilled men. Instead they've been recognized

ABOVE *Keeping his eye in. Charlie Smith checks the washbacks.*

TASTING NOTES

Glenkinchie 10-year-old 43%ABV
Grassy, fresh nose with a little lemon peel livening up the palate. Very fresh and clean.
* * *

Glenkinchie Distiller's Edition Amontillado finish 43%ABV
Grassy with a hint of sulphur/burnt match and roasted almond. Soft and gentle with an almost syrupy start then the fresh-mown grass gives it a lift. Gentle. * * *

UDV bottles two other Lowland malts. Bladnoch 10-year-old (40%ABV) has a delicate, almost minty nose, with a hint of caramelized orange and hay. Bladnoch is up and running again under new management.
* * *

The triple-distilled Rosebank 12-year-old (43%ABV) has a complex, aromatic nose with green grass, apple, lemon grass and an undercurrent of bracken/hay-accented fruit. Wonderfully balanced, with some smoke on the palate leading to a huge lift of sweet fruit and acacia honey. With the reopening of the Forth & Clyde Canal, on which it stands, there's a good chance whisky will be made here once again. * * *(*)

as skilled for the first time. In the past there was no room for initiative – there was a hell of a lot of latent talent that went unrecognized.'

But for Charlie and Jim there's no substitute for experience, which Charlie demonstrates as he peers into the wooden washbacks. 'You can look at the bubbles and tell the stage of the ferment,' he explains. 'At the start there's a creamy foam and small bubbles, then in the first 24 hours the speed of the bubbles increases. Then the head dies and you get big, soapy ones; then after 45 hours they die and it starts sizzling at the edges. It's down to the eye, so you can see the problem as soon as it happens. A lot of the job comes down to sensing when things aren't right.'

It reinforces the belief at Glenkinchie in balance, between old and new workers,

between tradition and innovation. 'What if the still does something strange?' asks Jim. 'If someone has never seen carryover he won't know what to do. Only an experienced stillman will know.' As Charlie adds: 'If you've driven skill and experience out of the system, where does the blame lie if something goes wrong? We should always have progress, but we'll always need experience'.

We dismiss blends without a second thought; after all, malt is what is interesting. But a good blend is as complex and fascinating a drink as any malt. Blends are the workhorses of the industry, the brands that still account for 90 per cent of the world's Scotch sales. Paradoxically, maybe that's why no-one talks about them, or understands how they are made: the fact that many folk still think there's a Johnnie Walker distillery is the fault of an industry which hasn't talked about the art and creativity of the unsung heroes and heroines in the blending rooms.

In the mid-19th century Scotland was emerging as a major industrial power. Its cities were growing and innovation was in the air. Whisky tapped right into it: it was the fuel for the workers, it was an opportunity for the new entrepreneurial middle class and for inventors such as Robert Stein and Aeneas Coffey.

Until the 1850s, grain whisky was either sold on its own or onto gin distillers in England, where it would be flavoured and redistilled (a practice that continues

BLENDED
SCOTCH

today). Then, in 1853, Usher's Old Vatted Glenlivet mingled the light-flavoured grain with the big malts and a new middle ground opened up.

The early blenders were mostly respectable grocers and wine merchants, men like John Dewar, Arthur Bell, Matthew Gloag, the Chivas brothers and John Walker. It was their sons, however, who perfected and then started marketing their creations across the globe, with astonishing verve and impudence.

Their success in persuading the world that it needed to drink blended whisky unleashed a new and powerful business, headed by innovators like the Dewar brothers, Alexander Walker, Peter Mackie and James Buchanan, blenders and marketeers who laid the foundations for the famous blends we know today.

Prohibition and Irish independence were new opportunities. Blends were unstoppable until the 1970s when, perhaps arrogant in their assumption that people would always drink blended Scotch, firms failed to connect with a new generation who preferred vodka. Today, there is a revival – mainly in southern Europe – but blends have lost their lustre. It's time to take them seriously again.

A blended Scotch is a mix of malt and grain whiskies, but what is grain whisky? Initially it was created to satisfy the demands of Lowland distillers for a low-cost, light-flavoured spirit produced in large volumes. For that we have to thank Robert Stein and Aeneas Coffey for inventing a 'continuous' still. Although continuous (or column) stills have become more advanced, Coffey's basic principle has remained in place.

These days most Scotch grain distillers will use wheat or corn, which is crushed and cooked with some malted barley (for its saccharine properties) fermented and then pumped into the top of the still. At the same time, steam is pumped in to the bottom of the still. This rises, meeting the cool worts as it descends over perforated plates, stripping off the alcoholic vapours and lifting them upwards. Water and alcohol boil at different temperatures and so do congeners, and as the vapours rise these components begin to separate (or 'fractionate'). The column can therefore separate everything except the higher (more delicate) alcohols, which are condensed on average at around 90%ABV.

It is the blender's job to take the mature grains and malts and combine them into a consistent blend. This will be built on an unchanging core of specific malts and grains which are supported by a changing cast of other malts, each of them bringing flavour, texture and bulk to the blend. Sounds simple? Well it isn't: the more you investigate the more fascinating the whole process becomes. Let them explain …

UDV
(UNITED DISTILLERS
AND VINTNERS)
JOHNNIE WALKER∘J&B∘BELL'S

One of the Scotch whisky industry's greatest secrets sits at the foot of the Ochil Hills. You may notice some warehouses close to the road as you drive past, but it's more likely that your eyes will be drawn to Dumyat's crags or the phallic thrust of the Wallace Monument on the near horizon. UDV's Blackgrange site does not draw attention to itself, there's nothing to indicate that there's close to 3 million casks of whisky quietly maturing in 49 blocks of warehouses. The scale is awesome. You are dwarfed by the

massive black warehouses, your imagination struggles to picture what a billion bottles of whisky looks like.

Whisky is big, we know that but you only realise how big when you drive down the avenues of Blackgrange. In the disgorging plant they are emptying up to 10,000 casks a week, at times the components for five different blends may be going out the same day.

Now imagine being in charge not just of all this maturing stock, but also in charge of the new make coming out of UDV's 27 malt and 2 grain distilleries. That's Turnbull Hutton's job. If you want to understand how a major blend is put together, ask Turnbull (UDV's operations director) and UDV's inventory and supply director, Christine Wright.

For Turnbull, putting together a blend doesn't start with assembling components in the lab or the disgorging hall, it begins when he gets the sales projections from UDV's sales force. Every salesman expects his brand to grow, he's staking his career prospects on it. Thankfully, the production side have seen it before and temper their enthusiasm, 'fuelled by many years of cynicism' as Turnbull puts it. No wonder he has a reputation for irascibility.

His job is to balance the sales forecasts, set production levels to supply the fillings for all the blends and work out the demand in terms of stock requirements. The whisky trade is always flying blind to a certain extent. The whisky you make today can't be used until it's three years old, you may be storing some to be used in 18 to 25 years time, as blends contain whiskies from a large range of ages. The aim is to get as close to a balance between supply and demand as possible. Get it too short and you have to

buy on the open market, make too much (as happened in the late 1970s) and you end up having to close distilleries.

The bottom line is if you don't get your projections right, it affects distilleries, puts people out of work and can affect style. The blender looks for balance in a blend, the operations director looks for balance in a distillery. 'I've got to interpret their forecasts and balance them with stock levels and production capability in order not to just turn the gas up or down at a distillery,' Turnbull explains. 'If you run on a normal regime and things are slow you can extend the silent season. If you start running longer ferments or run the stills hard and fast then you change the character'.

Once the operations and blending team has calculated the total production figures it can then start looking at the requirements of specific brands. The Johnnie Walker Black Label blend you are making today involves having got the planning right 12 or more years ago. To ensure that they can sell the estimated volumes of the same blend in 12 years time means that the right volumes of the core whiskies are being made this year and are made in the right style, put in the right wood and aged in the right warehouses.

To ensure consistency, the UDV blenders have blocked out nine different categories of malts, from Heavy Highland 'Heavier', through Light Highland 'Heavier', Speyside 'Light' to Islay and Lowland. Within each of those categories there are further

JOHNNIE WALKER *The world's top selling blended Scotch started life in John Walker's Kilmarnock grocer's shop in the 1880s. By 1908 his grandsons had registered Johnnie Walker as a trademark, and allied by clever marketing – and consistently high-quality blending – it was soon a world player. Black Label is still the blend to beat.*

TASTING NOTES

Johnnie Walker Red Label
The nose mixes light toffee peat smoke and fresh wood notes. Fresh and vivacious, it packs a crunchy, lightly peaty punch on the palate. ✳✳✳(✳)

Black Label 12-year-old
Gorgeously complex: perfume, peat and peaches in honey, soft grain and leather all in harmony. Silky and multi-layered on the palate, it balances a huge range of seductive flavours beautifully. ✳✳✳✳✳

Gold Label 18-year-old 43%ABV
Another stunner: richer than Black, with a hint of sea air and honey/beeswax. A complex palate of iced biscuits, ozone and rich malt. ✳✳✳✳✳

Blue Label
Peat fires smoulder in the glass and lead to a slowly unfolding palate, with all manner of dark truffle flavours: smoke, orange and bitter chocolate. Deep and profound – but is it worth the money? ✳✳✳✳

subdivisions into different classes, as well as into family styles of mature malt. Mapping out these different categories and styles allows blenders to interplay different components.

'Within Walker, for example, there are certain building blocks: a percentage of Islay, a percentage of Heavy Highland,' says Turnbull. 'If you've got the Walker building blocks right: Lagavulin, Cardhu and Heavy/Medium Highland, the fact you might be replacing Aberfeldy with something else isn't an issue.' As Christine adds: 'Within the 'recipe' there's a core that you don't alter, but behind it all are categories and sub-sections which are interchangeable. The art is knowing what substitutes to make and recognising the core malts from our own production units'.

What's often difficult for an outsider to grasp about blending is that there is no fixed recipe. 'There's a lot of tunes you can play,' says Turnbull. 'There's an average age for a blend, but you can hit that average in a lot of ways without changing the blend's flavour.' Bell's 8-year-old for example doesn't just have 8-year-old whiskies in it. This is where the skill of the blender comes into play. Knowing the brand style – light for J&B, rich for Walker – gives the blender an idea of how to use different ages, cask types and components – and what can be substituted.

'We know the minimum acceptable age for Walker Red is five years and Black is 12, but all the blends will have a top dressing of older malts,' says Turnbull. 'A blend like

BELOW *The art of blending hasn't changed at all down through the years.*

ABOVE *Chairman of the J&B board (1831–71), Alfred Brooks.*

J&B *This blend was created for top London wine merchants Justerini & Brooks in 1933, although the firm had been dealing in whiskies since 1768, and blending its Club Blend for private customers since 1884. Made specifically to suit the post-Prohibition American palate, J&B soon rose to become the second-largest selling blend in the world, and in recent years has spearheaded the whisky boom in Spain.*

TASTING NOTES

J&B
Very pale and delicate, with a hint of sweetness mixed with fragrant malt. Silky green fruits and hay on the palate. Ultra-light. ✳✳

Walker Red therefore can have grains of between four and six years of age and malts between five and ten. So, if the sales forecasts are out, there are ways in which older stock can be blended into the brand without affecting the style'.

All of this means having an in-depth knowledge of what each distillery's character is and how it matures in all the different casks you are putting it into. It also means ensuring that the distillery character is retained. There's no sense in running all your distilleries to the same regime and ending up with one style of whisky – as happened with Bell's prior to being bought by UD. 'We've spent lots of time working out what is the optimum character for, say, Clynelish,' says Christine, 'and had to replace the sludge [see pages 18–19] to ensure the character remained the same. The same happened with Dalwhinnie when we took the worms out.' (See pages 56–57.)

There are some distilleries which are capable of producing more than one style of whisky. 'Caol Ila [a significant player in Bell's and Walker blends] is one that excites me,' says Christine. 'I love that whisky! It's a superb Islay when you peat it, but unpeated it makes a great Highland malt in the Cragganmore/Clynelish mould. It's a style we make every year.' There's also a human element in this. 'Making the unpeated style not only helps us in terms of stocks, but it keeps Islay going,' she adds. 'Heavily-peated Islay whiskies are difficult to salt away in a blend at times of surplus. You can't just shove them in to use them up, so the fact that Caol Ila can make a great unpeated malt means it will keep producing no matter what ... and keep people in a job'.

Caol Ila is an exception though. Most distilleries are stubborn individuals. 'If we seriously wanted to change Mortlach could we do it?' she asks. 'No, you'd get a corrupted spirit. We always have to keep within the parameters of what the distillery character is'.

It's a polite way of responding to criticisms that the bigger the firm the more likely it is that all their whiskies will taste the same. Ask Turnbull the same question and he

visibly twitches. 'People think if you're big you don't care about quality and all the whisky is the same,' he says. 'In reality, our size has allowed us to do the opposite. We're more aware than anybody that we need the character of the 27 distilleries to come through. The Walker, Bell's or J&B character is paramount. We won't kill the goose that laid the golden egg'.

But there's no doubt that the in-depth research done by UDV into new make character, distillery character and wood ageing has made the bean counters in head office question the logic of one firm having 27 malt distilleries and two grain plants (and a 50 per cent share in another). After all, with all this research, isn't it possible to take a more cost-effective option and make all the malts and blends on one site? It's what the rest of the world does.

Turnbull's heard it all before. 'I'm always having to deal with people parachuting into this industry with smart ideas,' he sighs. 'They assume they're dealing with a bunch of numpties who have never had a good idea in their puff for the last 100 years.' So he called their bluff. 'I said, fine, let's build the biggest f—in' distillery in the world. There's just one drawback, you'll have an oil refinery and I don't see many tourists going to Grangemouth. Whisky sells because of the romance'.

Scratch any whisky person and a romantic soul peers out. These people have a passion for their job and their product. The men

BELL'S *Perth wine merchant Arthur Bell started blending in the 1860s, but it was his son 'AK' who first sold the whisky as Bell's in 1904. Still the UK's largest-selling whisky, its reputation suffered during the 1970s when overproduction brought quality crashing down. Relaunched as an 8-year-old in 1994, it is unrecognizable as the bad old whisky it briefly became.*

TASTING NOTES

Bell's 8-year-old
Mellow, fragrant nose with good depth of flavour. Some fruit cake, light perfume, leather, cocoa and cereal. Soft and chewy. Take time to rediscover it. ✳✳✳✳(✳)

RIGHT *Wine merchant Arthur Bell started blending in the 1860s.*

emptying thousands of casks in the disgorging hall, working in the vast warehouses, the coopers in the noisy, steamy joke-filled cooperage are the unsung heroes of the industry.

As for Christine, ask her about Walker and she becomes positively poetic. 'Walker Red is cheeky and in your face, Black is gorgeous, Blue is positively luxurious. They've all got that Islay thread and a different interplay of lingering flavours. Christ! I'm sounding like someone from marketing!"

The bottom line is that in Johnnie Walker and J&B they have two of the greatest blends in the world. To be able to produce them in such volumes and retain such high quality standards is an incredible feat. But who gives them a second thought? 'We've concentrated on malts for 10 years now,' says Christine. 'Classic Malts helped grow the market and that's great, but now it's time to make that link from them into the blends. We've got to recognize blends for what they're worth. I'm proud of these brands, they're not faceless products'.

LEFT *Whisky on ice has always been popular.*

BELOW *The Americans soon fell in love with blends.*

BLACK & WHITE *James Buchanan was one of blending's greatest characters and the man who, from the 1880s onwards, brought blended Scotch to the attention of the English middle classes – thanks to his creation of a lighter style of blend, which he renamed Black & White, in 1904. Once a major player for DCL, it's now sadly rather lost in UDV's massive portfolio.*

TASTING NOTES

Black & White
A hint of heather on the light nose, with plenty of fresh grain and light smoke. A crunchy almond centre with some mint toffee and a hint of smoke mid-way through. ✳✳✳

WHITE HORSE *Created by Sir Peter Mackie, the despotic, eccentric blender (and owner of Lagavulin), White Horse always wore its Islay heart on its sleeve, until recently. Now repositioned as a 'fighting' blend, it has been toned down slightly to appeal to a new audience.*

TASTING NOTES

White Horse
Some ripe apple and a hint of smoke on the nose. The palate has an immediate whack of turf/peat. Dries out in the middle, then broadens and becomes quite sweet. ✳✳(✳)

HIGHLAND
GROUSE○BLACK BOTTLE

Ask the Edrington Group's master blender, John Ramsay, what makes his drams different and he immediately proposes marriage. In the whisky-making sense, of course. Marriage used to be normal practice for blenders: before bottling, malts and grains would be brought together for a period of mingling. Most firms have abandoned the art, but Edrington sticks to the old ways, marrying its blends for six months and at reduced strength.

'The bean counters in most firms decided it wasn't helping the bottom line,' says John. 'But we ran an exercise to see if we were getting a benefit from marrying, and we were.' It's all down to maximizing flavour.

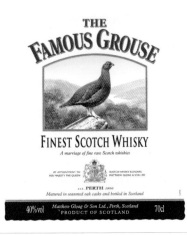

FAMOUS GROUSE *Perth wine merchant William Gloag started blending whiskies in the 1860s, to warm the cockles of the huntin', shootin', fishin' set. In 1896 his nephew, Matthew, created The Famous Grouse. It remained a little-known classic until the 1970s, but since then has become Scotland's favourite dram, number two in the UK, and is spreading its wings into export.*

TASTING NOTES

The Famous Grouse
A fat, juicy, succulent nose with a hint of menthol, lavender and a drift of smoke. Lovely weight on the palate, which is sweet, lightly spiced and tinged with peat. ****(*)

'When you add water to cask-strength malt, some components become unstable,' he continues. 'We give that time to settle, which means we can give the final blend a light filtration. If you don't do this you'll have to give it a harder filtration to get that stability – and then you lose some flavour'.

The process is made more complicated by his insistence on marrying blocks of blends. 'We'll combine malts and grains; reduce, marry and have Blend One,' he explains. 'Then we repeat the exercise and get Blends Two to Four. When it comes to bottling, rather than just using all of Blend One and then moving on, we'll use some from each batch. It's a form of whisky solera'.

But we skip ahead. Edrington's brands (which include Famous Grouse, Cutty Sark – which they blend for Berry Bros – Lang's Supreme and Black Bottle) start their lives as the new make samples from a host of distilleries, and are nosed by John every day. Then, like every blender, he has to work out how much new make to lay down, to satisfy potential demand for any of the brands many years down the line. It's this ability to assess new make and mature spirit that sets blenders apart.

John can stick his nose in a glass of Glenrothes 5-year-old from sherry wood and know if it fits 'the wee picture in my head', and also how that whisky will behave when combined with thirty others. While some of us may be able to pick out a few malts at a blind tasting, a blender knows not just what it is but whether it fits within the right parameters according to age and wood. It's an awesome ability, but this modest man hasn't allowed it to go to his head.

These blends are very different creatures: they don't just have different core malts, the wood recipe has also been carefully plotted. The sherry wood in the delicate Cutty comes from American oak; the richer Lang's uses Spanish oak and Grouse uses both. 'You want a fragrant sweet aroma in Cutty, so you use American wood and a Speyside malt like

different grains: some for commercial reasons, but also to give different characters in the blend. We'll use Strathclyde when it's younger, as it matures quicker. North British ages well, so it will be used in older blends – it also rounds out the wood influence on older whiskies.

'A blend is a bit like a pasta with sauce,' John concludes. 'The grain is the pasta, edible but bland, and the malts are the sauce – a bit strong on their own, but together they're a great combination.'

Tamdhu for sweetness, with some Bunnahabhain for freshness. Grouse is Speyside-based as well, but there is a lot of influence from Highland Park and the mix of sherry from Spanish and American wood'.

He uses a very Scottish analogy to describe the art of blending. 'It's like putting together a good soccer team. You need a strong central core, then you can tack the stars around that. It's useless if you haven't got that central core right.' But the unsung, hard-working midfielder in all the Edrington blends is North British grain. 'We use

CUTTY SARK *First made in 1923 by London wine merchants Berry Bros & Rudd, Cutty Sark was specifically made as a light-flavoured blend that would appeal to the American market, even though Prohibition was in force. It was smuggled into the United States by one Captain William McCoy and became so popular that people began demanding 'the real McCoy' as their choice of bootleg liquor.*

TASTING NOTES

Cutty Sark
Gentle, light nose with oat, butter, icing sugar and some delicate raspberry. A mix of cream and grass, with a touch of lemon sherbet on the finish. ∗∗∗

BLACK BOTTLE *Originally conceived by Aberdeen tea merchant Gordon Graham in the 1870s, Black Bottle passed through many different hands before landing in Highland Distillers' lap in 1995. John Ramsay has since reformulated it to be 'the malt with the heart of Islay' and uses all seven Islay malts in the blend. It's a brand to watch.*

TASTING NOTES

Black Bottle 10-year-old
Islay personified: ozone, ginger, ripe fruit and ginger. With water, an intense smoky perfume leaps out, then mingles with soft cakey fruit before a blast of salt-spray halfway through. Stunning. ∗∗∗∗∗

ALLIED

BALLANTINE'S∘TEACHER'S

The journey from Glasgow to Allied Distillers' Dumbarton headquarters takes you along an invisible line dividing the industrial central belt and the rural Highlands. On one side lies the summit of Ben Lomond, iced with the first snow of winter, and on the other Allied's redbrick grain distillery, which dominates the Dumbarton skyline. It's the perfect setting for a blender, encapsulating the art of melding the romantic Highland malts with the Clyde-built grains. Given the proximity of the grain distillery, there's little surprise that when you ask Allied's master blender Robert Hicks for the secret behind Ballantine's, he talks about grain before anything else.

'One of the key elements that makes Ballantine's different to all other blends is that it must always have a minimum percentage of Dumbarton maize whisky in the blend,' he says. 'There is something about grain whisky made from maize that adds sweetness to a blend'. Robert is never short of an opinion, but he backs up his Glaswegian garrulousness with ample proof, rushing around the sample room, pulling out whiskies and shoving them at you. 'No-one understands grain … everyone talks about malts, but unless you have that grain base you've nothing to build on'.

Robert feels that the blend of grains sitting on that sweet Dumbarton bedrock is as important as the malts. 'You need that correct mix,' he says, bringing out samples of silky-sweet Dumbarton maize, sulphury North British maize and sharp Strathclyde wheat. 'You can play as many tunes with

BALLANTINE'S *George Ballantine was another of the great grocer-blenders, this time based in Glasgow, who began blending whiskies in the late 19th century. In 1922 the firm started supplying the thirsty Prohibition-struck US – often through Canada, where the blend caught the attention of Hiram Walker, who promptly bought the firm and built the elegant grain distillery in Dumbarton whose whisky still acts as the foundation stone for the blends. Now part of Allied Domecq, Ballantine's is a massive brand in Europe.*

TASTING NOTES

Ballantine's Finest
A cream toffee-sweet nose, with gentle grassy notes. Clean and soft with a crisp mid-palate, it's a sound standard blend. ✳✳✳

Gold Seal 12-year-old
A creamy nose, with hints of smoke and high-toned perfume. Well-balanced there's a light tingle of grain on the soft finish. ✳✳✳(✳)

17-year-old
Magnificent, with soft grain pulsing through aromas of coffee extract/chicory , walnut, cake mix, smoke and lavender. A multi-layered, chewy palate with vanilla, peat and spun sugar. A powerful, seductive dram. ✳✳✳✳✳

30-year-old
Packed with rancio notes: leaf mould, mushroom, floor polish, cigar boxes and Bourbon-like woody notes. Strangely attenuated to start with, it moves into chocolate, burnt orange and a rich peat surge. Bags of character, but a little too woody for many. ✳✳✳✳

ABOVE *A Glaswegian always gets his priorities right.*

RIGHT *The spirit of Ballantine's.*

IT'S WHAT'S INSIDE THAT COUNTS

grains as you can with the malts. They aren't there to cheapen the blend or drag down malt ... and as for them not ageing? Rubbish.' He pushes over a glass of gorgeous, luxuriant 15-year-old Dumbarton grain. 'Come on, tell me that isn't a superb whisky'. I can't. It is. He's right.

Once he has the foundation of grains in place, the malty walls of the Ballantine's house-including Miltonduff and Glenburgie-go up. 'Then you can flesh it out, and it doesn't matter what with, as long as the core

eight to ten elements are the same'. Robert points out that a blender looks at malts in a different way to a consumer. 'I'm not thinking of malts as drinks on their own,' he says, 'but the way they react with each other. Some will give you power, others are moderators. The art of blending is achieving that balance and interaction. That's something you can't teach, it can only come with experience'.

Like most blenders, he's dismissive of the outsider's need to know exactly which whiskies he uses, and of people's subsequent claims that they can detect specific players in the blend. 'I was trained never to use a standard reference point,' he says. 'Putting a blend together isn't about copying what's in a bottle: you have to learn the whiskies, develop a picture of what Ballantine's 'is'; which is soft, sweet, round and smooth. There are no jagged edges, no individual malt comes through. We're creating a flavour package and we make it through experience and knowledge'.

So there is no such thing as a fixed recipe for Ballantine's, Teacher's or any of the other Allied blends. It seems paradoxical, but to maintain consistency of style and flavour you have to keep changing. 'If you stick religiously to a formula, your whisky will vary from spring to autumn,' says Robert. 'The hard and fast recipe is in our minds; it's the memory of smell'.

His assistant Sandy Hyslop takes up the point. 'It's a misconception that you can tell what whiskies are in a blend. There are 20 ages, 4 different types of casks, and 6 different fills – and different grains'. Having such a range of variables means that their work doesn't start when the casks of whisky are ready to be blended; they must be involved in every aspect of production.

'A blender has to be a perfectionist,' says Robert. 'He has to be finicky and have the integrity and guts to say: 'No, that's not right'. We want a sample from every tank of new make sent to us before it goes into wood and every cask is nosed before it is disgorged.

'The blend is nosed when it's put together, when it goes to packaging, after it's filtered and once it's in the bottle, and it can be rejected at any stage. Every single piece of new equipment that comes into contact with whisky-whether it's a tube, a gasket or a hose-has to be tested and cleared by Sandy or myself before it can be installed. That's where integrity comes in, saying to people: 'that ain't going in.' You have to be a perfectionist in this game. Jack Goudy [his predecessor] used to say it takes 30 years to build a brand and one bad batch to ruin it'.

In order to secure the correct flavour package Robert is ultimately in control of the distillation parameters at Allied's plants. At his insistence the stills at Ardmore [and the currently mothballed Glendronach, both core malts in Teacher's] have remained coal-fired. 'If you changed the firing at Ardmore you'd start having trouble,' he says. 'It's more expensive and it's dirtier, but I'm not willing to change the character to make a saving – and I can show the bosses samples to prove my point'.

Only when you see the big picture do you realize how daunting is the blender's job, and how blended whisky is undervalued. For Robert, blends are the great leveller, the

TEACHER'S *William Teacher was a Glaswegian blender who established his blend through his 'dram shops', which only sold his whisky! A popular blend in England, it was another old-style brand which fell on hard times during the 1970s.*

TASTING NOTES

Teacher's Highland Cream
A ripe, meaty nose mixing toffee with good, smoky notes. There's a smoky belch to start on the palate, then the toffee comes back with a spicy, grainy undercurrent. ∗∗∗(∗)

LEFT *William Teacher established his brand through so-called 'dram shops'.*

RIGHT *The oldest known labelled bottle of scotch whisky.*

BELOW *Guardian of his brands, Allied blender Robert Hicks.*

whisky that everyone should enjoy. 'It would be ridiculous if I walked into a pub with you, went straight to the bar and ordered you a Laphroaig without asking you what you liked,' he says. 'I'll happily buy a blend and know you'll enjoy it. That's why blending was invented, to make whisky accessible'.

Robert maintains that blending is not just about maintaining a consistent style, but being aware of the human history and heritage contained in any brand. Blenders are, in their own way, guardians of their brands, passing their knowledge down through the years. Robert is only the fourth master blender of Ballantine's this century and can trace his lineage back to Sir Peter Mackie, the creator of White Horse.

Robert is now training Sandy to be the next guardian, but Sandy realizes how important it is not to become a cardboard cutout of your predecessor; you must bring your own personality to the proceedings. 'This isn't a job you do for three or four years and then say: 'That was nice, now I'll try marketing'. A blender is in the job for life,' he says. 'I'm currently laying down whisky that I'll use when I'm 60. You've got to see it through and you need continuity.' On cue, Robert finishes the sentence. 'In whisky, that continuity comes from production. The other side of the industry is just a job: on this side you have to have passion. The guys in the distillery are the first line of defence, they have to get it right; the warehousing has to be right; we have to get it right. It's a mix of everything'.

CHIVAS

Trying to get a blender to explain what his or her job involves is never easy. Not because they are secretive, far from it. They're almost relieved to have a chance to tell their story.

CHIVAS *The Chivas brothers owned a high-class grocery business in Aberdeen and started blending whiskies (for, among others, the Royal household) in the 1880s. Regal appeared at the turn of the 20th century and was another light Speyside-dominant blend to make it big in the United States during Prohibition. It was bought by the Canadian distiller (and one-time bootlegger) Sam Bronfman in 1949 and is still a major player in the US and Far East markets.*

TASTING NOTES

Chivas Regal 12-year-old
Deceptive weight behind the apparently light mix of grass, apples and cereal on the nose. A grassy, almost mossy start to the palate, it crisps up deliciously mid-palate. ✴✴✴(✴)

18-year-old
A magnificent mélange of currant leaf, orange pulp/peach cobbler, barley malt and turfy smoke. The palate explodes with flavour, but always in that elegant, restrained family style. ✴✴✴✴✴

Oldest
The finest in the range. Peatier still, with a rich, complex mix of citrus notes (tangerine, lemon) heather, fruit and spicy grain. Stunning. ✴✴✴✴✴

It's just that the intricacies of blending are so complex that strange analogies have to be employed: orchestras, football teams, actors, cars, cakes, houses – all appear in the blender's lexicon.

Colin Scott, master blender at Chivas Brothers, is a master of the art. Created by a firm of high-class Aberdonian grocers who began blending whiskies in the 1840s, Chivas Regal has been Seagram's flagship Scotch since 1949. It is Colin, however, who has overseen the recent explosion of Chivas brands, including the superb 18-year-old and the awesome Oldest.

Colin feels it's important not to get hung up over numbers. 'How many malts and grains go into the blend isn't important,' he says. 'What is important is always having Chivas in the glass.' The one constant is Strathisla. 'Making a Chivas blend is like building a house; with malts as the bricks, grains as the mortar and Strathisla as the foundation. Chivas Regal is one shape of house, 18-year-old is grander and Oldest is a castle!'

They may be individual brands, but there is a distinct family resemblance. 'The brands have a thread running through them ... richness, smoothness and roundness of flavours. You use different bricks to change the flavour profile, while retaining the character,' says Colin. 'That means manipulating the range of available flavours (different malts, grains, wood types, ages) and creating different but similar teams. Chivas 18- isn't 12-year-old aged for a further 6 years, it's a different team.'

To make matters more interesting, each team is in a constant state of flux. 'Consumers don't want to see character or quality alter, but to preserve them you must make changes,' urges Colin. 'If you have one pot of whiskies to use in a blend, you must always also have another pot which though it contains different whiskies will have the same flavour as the first. Because you know what is in each of the pots, you know what any differences are and can therefore find ways to narrow any gap between them.

'That second pot is like footballers sitting on the bench. We know how they perform,

Drink responsibly. (But you know that.)

rise and fall, but the style and character remains the same.

'It's about teamwork and having a passion for whisky,' says Colin. 'Everyone from the distilleries to packaging is involved. And that's not just our distilleries: we rely on everyone in the industry to have the same passion'.

Gaining access to the mind of any blender leaves you baffled as to why blends are derided as boring, one-dimensional commodities. 'As an industry we didn't used to talk about blends,' says Colin. 'They aren't so easy to understand as malts, those great characters with huge flavour profiles. But because we have these different flavours, we can create an even greater one by blending them. A blend isn't just one individual, idiosyncratic character – it has complexity.' He giggles again, wrestling with the final analogy. 'Chivas has all these different flavours, it's a wave of flavours. That's how to look at it ... the perfect wave'.

so our job is to make sure that whatever ones we use, they'll make Chivas. The difference between 12- and 18-year-old is that the gap between the two pots widens'. Colin regards blending as working in a state of perpetual fluidity. It's only when you do it yourself – and ruin a blend's character by adding a touch too much of one whisky – that you can begin to understand the complexities of his job. Distilleries come and go, peating levels

DEWAR'S∘BNJ

Dewar's was the first blend to be advertised by electric sign and the first to produce a cinema advertisement – both products from the fertile mind of the irrepressible Tommy Dewar. By 1894 he had conquered the United States, established a global distribution network and created a following for his White Label brand which has stayed loyal ever since.

Although it was sold to Bacardi after the UDV merger, master blender Tom Aitken approaches his work in the same way as he has always done. Consistency is his mantra: 'The consumer wants his or her blend to be exactly the same every time,' he argues. 'The first role of any master blender is to lay down enough whiskies to ensure that consistency.' And he dare not change anything. 'When we

changed the label, people complained about the quality of the whisky, even though we hadn't altered a thing. That label change had altered their perception of the brand – that's how closely people become attached to it'.

Malt from Aberfeldy remains at the core of the blend, but Tom is quick to dismiss the idea that the more malts there are in a blend, the better it is. 'One grain and one malt blend will be a disaster, but equally having 50 malts won't make the blend any better. The key is having consistency and balance'.

Unlike Dewar's, which has been a global brand since the 1890s, Glenmorangie's Bailie Nicol Jarvie is a hidden gem. Paradoxically, if you look at the two labels, it's BNJ which would appear to be the Victorian classic; it's evocative of a time when blends were the sophisticated drink. Indeed, it's a pretty sophisticated dram. The sole grain is from North British, there's a 60 per cent malt content and those malts (with Glenmorangie making a rare appearance) are between eight and 17 years of age – and there's only eight of them. 'The quality of the malts gives the character, not the quantity,' explains Glenmorangie's Craig Taylor. 'We're using malts purely for their character, not to bulk up the blend'. It's a glorious success and if malt aficionados consider blends as being beneath them, they should try this. Instant conversion awaits.

DEWAR'S *Tommy Dewar knew what he was doing when he set off around the world in 1893. If James Buchanan (see page 93) was the gentleman, Tommy was the prankster and he soon established White Label as the biggest-seller in the US. When UD and IDV merged, Dewar's was forcibly sold off, and was snapped up by Bacardi. Quite what its secretive new owner is planning no-one knows.*

TASTING NOTES

Dewar's White Label
Light, with good malty notes and a touch of lemon meringue pie and honey. Soft and easy, with a lemon/ginger malt-driven mid-palate. ***

BNJ *Named after a fictional character in Walter Scott's Rob Roy, Bailie Nicol Jarvie first appeared in the 1860s, but was reformulated in 1994 by owner Glenmorangie, though it still sports a wonderfully anachronistic Victorian label.*

TASTING NOTES

Bailie Nicol Jarvie
Medium weight, with flowers, vanilla, pears and apples on the nose. Very subtle and rounded, bursting with malty flavours. Superb length. *****

GRANT'S

As the whisky industry continues to consolidate, the days of family-owned distiller/blenders is fast becoming a memory. William Grant & Sons is one of the few noble exceptions, proving that a family firm compete with the UDVs of this world by being as self-sufficient as possible.

Every firm uses its own malts as the core of its blends: Grant's can draw on the Dufftown triumvirate of Glenfiddich, Balvenie and Kininvie, although it still buys or exchanges over 40 other malts for its blends. Grant's also uses its own grain whisky from its distillery in Girvan, which it bottles as Black Barrel.

The need to keep as many of the fillings in-house was the rationale behind building Kininvie in 1990. Constructing a new distillery is always a slightly nervy experience, as you can never be 100 per cent certain how the malt will turn out, how it will mature or how it will behave in a blend. Thankfully, Grant's ever-modest master blender David Stewart is happy with Kininvie's performance so far. 'We built it to give us a fruity note for the blends,' he explains. 'I've been using it in Family Reserve for the past four years and eventually it may end up in the 12-year-old, though we still don't know what a 12-year-old Kininvie will be like'.

Kininvie's arrival doesn't mean the malts it replaces are immediately taken out of the blend, as the process is a gradual one involving constant balancing and rebalancing of flavours and components in the blends. What is certain is that Kininvie won't disturb the graceful, sweet and complex Grant's style; wherein David uses the clean, quick-maturing Girvan grain as a platform for some powerful interplay between the malts. While the Dufftown core remains the same in the Grant's range, he uses lighter malts in Clan McGregor and Family Reserve, and meatier players such as Cragganmore, Highland Park and The Macallan in older blends. 'There may be more malt in the older blends,' he says, 'but don't underestimate the grain. It does provide flavour as well'.

GRANT'S *One of the most famous families in whisky, the Grants had already built their Glenfiddich distillery three years prior to the launch of their blend – originally Standfast, now Family Reserve.*

TASTING NOTES

Grant's Family Reserve
A fragrant nose, mixing honey/lime blossom, pear and light smoke. Very soft toffee/vanilla start before a good, subtle interplay between malt and grain, and a crisp and deliciously nutty finish. ✳✳✳✳

LEFT *William Grant. His dynasty has stood fast for over 100 years.*

The precise origins of whisky remain a matter of conjecture and debate, best waged with a glass in hand and a long evening in front of you. But Ireland has the strongest claim. The secret of distillation was held by monks and Ireland was a beacon of culture and education during the Dark Ages, so it's entirely plausible that this isn't just the birthplace of whisky making – it's one of the most important early centres of distillation.

Some argue that early references to *aqua vitae* refer to distilled wine and not whiskey,

IRISH WHISKEY

but it seems slightly fanciful that in a country where distillation was known, alchemist-monks turning wine into brandy wouldn't have made the logical leap to do the same with beer – and develop whiskey. Alchemists, in their search for the essence of life itself, were inquisitive souls willing to distil anything – even swans and human brains – to reach their goal.

Regardless of the history debate, Ireland is undeniably an ideal country for whiskey making. There is soft, pure water, plentiful supplies of barley and in the past a rural population who found distilling a handy way to boost their income. By the end of the 18th century a split had emerged between the *poitín* made in the country and the town whiskies – often flavoured with roots and herbs – which had become fashionable not just in Dublin, but among 'polite' society in Paris and London. It was these urban distillers who won the battle for the soul of Irish whiskey, as the rural poor were targeted by lawmakers at the start of the 19th century. The mass temperance movement led by the charismatic priest Father Mathew also put paid to pubs and distilleries, while the Great Famine of 1845–49 slashed the amount of grain available for distilling, forced people off the land and into exile and sounded the death knell for the small rural distiller.

The moneyed distillers – John Jameson, John Power, George Roe and William Jameson's Marrowbone Lane operation in Dublin, and the Murphy brothers' grand Midleton distillery in County Cork – soon controlled the industry. They were so confident about the quality of their pot still whiskeys that when Robert Stein and the Irishman Aeneas Coffey perfected the continuous still these whiskey big guns fought an eloquent (though ultimately fruitless) battle against the new fangled 'silent spirit', arguing that it could not be called whiskey.

They were initially speaking from a position of power, and distilling on an epic scale – in virtual temples of whiskey making. Indeed, before blended Scotch burst onto the scene, Irish pot still was considered to be the finest whiskey in the world. In retrospect, however, the big names' failure to embrace the Coffey still was the first nail in their coffin. But where else did it all go wrong?

To begin with, America declared Prohibition and cut off Ireland's largest export market. The bootleggers started making 'bathtub Irish' and their reputation plummeted. The advent of independence then isolated Ireland from the British Empire, which accounted for a quarter of sales; then the Irish government, needing to raise quick revenue, hiked up taxes. Distillers went bust.

In 1966, Jameson, Power's and Cork Distillers joined forces to form Irish Distillers and in 1975 consolidated production in the space-age Midleton plant. When the last remaining distiller, Bushmills, was amalgamated into the group in 1973, Irish Distillers became the sole producer of Irish whiskey – most of it, incredibly, coming from one site.

Today, though, with the independent Cooley on the scene and a stunning range of new whiskeys emerging from Irish Distillers, there's a confidence that hasn't been seen since the start of the 20th century. To understand the intricacies of Irish whiskey making, it's best to listen to the unassuming people who have kept the quality standard flying through the long, hard years.

BUSHMILLS

Driving along the spectacular Antrim coast you can just tell that this is good whiskey-making country. Soft pasture land, small rivers, natural harbours and a people who know that good things take time. It's a land where legend and fact become easily blurred, where folk tales take on the mantle of truth. Who knows when whiskey was first made here? Some historians claim it started in 1276, though if the story of monks taking distilling with them when they went to convert the heathen Picts is true, it could be as far back at the 6th century. Authorization

was given for whiskey to be legally made in the county in 1608, allowing Bushmills to claim that it has been making the stuff since then – and laying the foundations for some mighty *craic* in 2008!

Bushmills is significantly different to the other two Irish distilleries and takes you back to a time when all of Ireland's whiskey only came from pot stills. There again, this being Ireland, it's also atypical of the traditional Irish pot-still style insofar as it doesn't use a mix of malted and unmalted barley. But it's not quite like a typical Scottish malt distillery as it uses triple distillation and unpeated malt – though so do Auchentoshan and Springbank's Hazelburn.

It's a complex process, as master distiller David Quinn explains. 'After distilling the low wines in the second [or feints] still we take the strong feints forward to a third distillation which gives us a distillate at around 84%ABV. The weak feints get recycled in the second distillation with the head and tails from the third. What we're doing is leaving behind the heavier aspects of the spirit and shifting the flavour balance to more fragrant, lighter, sweeter fruity character'.

The distillery is only a few miles from the Giant's Causeway, a weird outcrop of hexagonal basalt pillars that look like a monstrous pipe organ which, legend would have it, was the southern end of a bridge linking Ireland with Fingal's Cave on the Hebridean island of Staffa. In many ways Bushmills is a modern day bridge between two whisk(e)y-making cultures. 'There's a lot

TASTING NOTES

Black Bush
Sweet, toffee-like nose with plenty of sherry notes in evidence. The palate is silky and soft, balancing ripe malt, raisined sherry wood and rich fruitiness. *****

Bushmills 10-year-old
Clean and crisp, with apple blossom, clover and bran. Lightly creamy on the palate, with some almond paste and gentle grassiness on the finish. Pleasant and soft. ***

Bushmills Triple Wood
Ripe and full on the nose. A taste of molasses, then some raisin mixed with powerful, plummy fruits. Well balanced. ***(*)

of the tradition of Irish pot still whiskey making here,' says David. 'But by being a single malt we're moving into the Scottish tradition. Maybe we can claim that we take the best of both traditions! On a good day we can see Islay, it's only 16 miles, so that link has always been there – maybe starting with monks like St. Columba'. In more recent times, ex-manager Frank McHardy nipped across the sea to Campbeltown's Springbank distillery – no surprise he's behind the triple distilled, unpeated Hazelburn!

Where Bushmills differs from any Scottish distillery is by being home to blends as well as single malts – most importantly the magnificent Black Bush, a blend of 80 per cent Bushmills single malt and grain from Midleton. Bushmills follows the Irish Distillers' policy of using a high percentage of first-fill sherry and Bourbon wood, both of them wood types packed with powerful flavours. The fact that David's light distillate isn't drowned out by these big flavours is testimony to some high-class blending skills. 'Getting the correct balance is vital. You could argue that with a delicate spirit it's even more vital that you get that flavour in correct balance with the wood. It also means we have to have top-quality wood. You can spend all the time in the world making a good distillate and then lose it by using sub-standard cooperage.' This shows best in the Triple Wood, a single malt initially aged in ex-Bourbon and sherry wood for 16 years before the two elements are married together and then recasked into port pipes for up to a year. Innovative, modern, yet in touch with the past – just like David and his team.

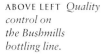

ABOVE LEFT *Quality control on the Bushmills bottling line.*

RIGHT *The Bushmills distillery. Bushmills is the bridge between Irish and Scottish whiskey making.*

IRISH DISTILLERS
JAMESON∘POWERS∘PADDY

The fact that there are only three distilleries in Ireland would suggest that this has always been a small-scale industry. Take time to visit the Old Jameson Distillery in Dublin or the Jameson Heritage Centre in Midleton, County Cork and another truth is immediately apparent. These are distilleries built on a grand scale. Both sites are long silent, but give a glimpse of a time when Irish whiskey rather than Scotch was the world's favourite style. No wonder distillers like Jameson and Power rejected the column still; the world wanted their pot-still whiskey. By the end of the 19th century, Jameson's Bow St. plant was employing 300 people and 2 million gallons were sleeping beneath the Dublin streets.

But history stepped in and five years after the formation of Irish Distillers, the Bow St.

splash of the water wheel which powered the plant.

Then in 1975 the wheel stopped, the largest pot still in the world (at 31,648 gallons big enough to hold a party in) produced its last spirit. But the ending of the old world ushered in a new one of high-tech whiskey making. 'New' Midleton, carefully hidden from the tourists' gaze, may look unimpressively industrial from the outside, but is the most remarkable distillery in the world.

So why haven't we heard about it? Maybe the industry had been so badly beaten up that it lost confidence in selling to the world. Until recently that is. Jameson is currently the fastest-growing whiskey brand in the world, new lines are appearing at a rate of knots. But we skip ahead.

LEFT *Queuing up. Jameson was one of the first truly global brands.*

BELOW *Casks of Jameson were stashed in warehouses throughout the centre of Dublin.*

site closed. Production was switched to Power's equally grand John's Lane distillery for three years, before the new plant at Midleton started up in 1975.

Much the same happened in Cork Distilleries' massive 'Old' Midleton distillery now (slightly confusingly) called The Jameson Heritage Centre. It's undoubtedly impressive, but like all silent distilleries, slightly sad and ghostly. Wandering round this vast plant you can imagine the scrape of the shovels in the malting barns, the creak of the pulleys, the hiss and rattle of the stills, the clatter of hooves in the cobbled courtyard, the cries and laughter of the men, the calming

How can you make 30-plus different whiskies (and gin and vodka) in one site? The few visitors who are allowed into the Midleton still room spend an age shaking their heads in wonder at the four massive pot stills sitting opposite the seven columns that shoot up to the roof. 'Effectively, what we have here is two distilleries rolled into one – a pot still/malt whiskey distillery and a column still light/grain whiskey distillery,' says master distiller Barry Crockett, looking down into the cavernous stillhouse. 'What's unique is the way the distillate streams can be diverted from the pot still side to the column still side, and vice versa. Actually, I can use any combination that takes my fancy!' In other words, he can make a triple distilled pot still spirit, or pot-column-pot, or column-pot-pot, or … well, you get the idea. Just through distillation, different flavour profiles are created.

There's more. 'The cut points for each component whiskey will vary,' he says. 'Say we're making one for Jameson 15-year-old. It will have a different cut point to the standard Jameson. Power's and Paddy will also have their own different cut points, distillation techniques – and mashbills.' Most of the pot still whiskeys use a percentage of unmalted barley – giving them a distinctive crunchy, spicy quality. 'It's hard to describe,' says

JAMESON *One of the great names in Irish distilling history, John Jameson was a Scot who established a distillery in Dublin's Bow Street in 1780. It became one of the major names in world whiskey, at the leading edge of distilling techniques and maturation. The Bow Street plant closed in 1971 and now all Jameson's is made in Midleton, County Cork.*

TASTING NOTES

Jameson
A generous, soft and slightly malty nose, with a crisp edge. Good intensity on the palate, with sherry notes and a creamily smooth finish. ✳✳✳(✳)

Jameson 1780
A generously-sherried nose, with an attractive lifted perfume. Sleek, but with a refreshing peanut brittle crunch mid-palate. ✳✳✳✳

Jameson's 15-year-old
Elegant and juicily ripe, like peaches in syrup, with a delicious crisp and spicy note on the nose. A wonderful interplay between light spices, hickory, lemon balm and juicy, cakey flavours. Gorgeously complex. A long finish, with Brazil nut/hazelnut, soft juicy fruit and lemon. Superb. ✳✳✳✳✳

POWERS *Another of the great Dublin distillers, John Power began distilling in 1791 and his John's Lane distillery was one of the greatest and grandest plants in Ireland. He was the first distiller to bottle his whiskey and the first to bottle miniatures. His brand is still Ireland's favourite.*

TASTING NOTES

Powers
Full and luscious, with masses of peachy fruit bursting out of the glass. Soft and unctuous, with a great balance between soft pulpy fruits and a crisp crunch from the unmalted barley ✳✳✳✳(✳)

Powers 12-year-old
Even more hedonistic, with a mix of rich fresh fruit and mouth-watering malt. Almost indecent in its plump richness. ✳✳✳✳(✳)

Crested 10
Technically part of the Jameson stable, with a weighty, malty nose leading to a broad sherried, even tarry palate that coats the mouth. Huge flavours and a long, elegant finish. ✳✳✳✳(✳)

Redbreast 12-year-old
The Crested 10 pales in comparison with this unblended pot still whiskey. Has a ripe sherried character with delicious cumin/lemon spiciness to liven the mouth up. ✳✳✳✳✳

master blender Barry Walsh. 'It has its own character, quite different to malted barley. Our pot still whiskey has certain perfumy oiliness – 'spicy' also crops up a lot.'

Whatever the right term may be, Barry Crockett through his subtle manipulation of mashbills, cut points and distillation techniques produces a huge range of triple-distilled whiskies. That though is only part of the story. To find how the next layer of flavour is laid on these new distillates you have to be taken around the warehouses by Brendan Monks and given a humorous, passionate explanation of Irish Distillers' wood policy.

By the late 1970s, the production team realized that, if they were to embark on a new quality-driven path for Irish whiskey, they would have to make some tough (and expensive) decisions. Fundamental to this was a comprehensive review of the wood policy. Over the next seven or eight years out went the knackered old barrels and in came a new quality-derived system. 'They had the vision,' says Brendan. 'They knew the only way for Irish whiskey to survive was to be obsessive about quality.' The research by Brendan and his team into sherry wood, Spanish oak, the use of first-fill barrels, matching the right wood to the distillate – predates the work done in Scotland, but has been largely ignored by the industry. 'Perhaps we just got on with the job and didn't blow our own trumpet,' says Brendan with a wry smile. 'But without being arrogant we do believe that we have led the world as far as wood research is concerned. It is the new frontier in whiskey making'.

The tight spec for each brand involves a very high percentage of first-fill sherry and Bourbon casks, all helping build layers of flavour and complexity to the whiskies. Inevitably, different types of cask will fit with certain brands. 'There's something magical about the marriage of the smoothly-flavoured pot still whiskey at the core of all Jameson whiskey and oloroso sherry wood,' says Barry Crockett. 'The old Jameson distillers certainly knew what they were at when they stipulated minimum levels of

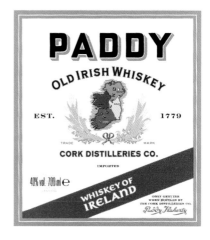

RIGHT *Barry Crockett, born at Midleton distillery and now running it.*

PADDY *Originally owned by Cork Distillers, this brand was named after their most famous salesman, Paddy Flaherty, who – by the cunning technique of buying a round for everyone in a bar – not only established his brand but had people asking for 'Paddy's whiskey'. Well, it was easier than asking for a glass of Cork Distilleries Company Old Irish Whiskey!*

TASTING NOTES

Paddy
The lightest of the main Irish Distillers' brands; slightly hot on the nose, with a touch of tangerine peel. A nice crunch on the palate, but a little lean. * *

sherry wood for their whiskey. We haven't changed a thing'.

The differences between the standard Jameson and the 15-year-old therefore starts at the distillate. They have the same mashbill, but the 15-year-old is cut to give it a more body so it will needs longer to mature. Though both are matured in a high percentage of first-fill sherry and Bourbon, the standard Jameson is blended with some light corn whiskey, the 15-year-old is all pot still.

All the barrels are aged standing on their ends in huge palletized warehouses. Brendan is quick to dismiss the argument that old dunnage warehouses maintained a constant temperature and allowed greater air movement. 'It hasn't made any noticeable change to the whiskey. The whiskey used to be stored wherever there was space in the old days – there was precious little air movement in those old tunnels under the Dublin streets!'

Barry Walsh's office sits on top of some of these old tunnels. The final member of the trio, he's been quietly working away for years and is now putting out some world-class new brands – proof not just of his skill, but the quality control exercised by Barry and Brendan down in County Cork.

You sometimes get a feeling that they mildly resent that people seem to believe that malt Scotch is the only way to make quality whiskey. They're far too nice to ever admit it though. Maybe Irish Distillers was too insular to tell the world what it was up to, maybe it was simply playing the long game. 'We feel that Irish whiskey is on the up and up,' says Barry Walsh. 'It's a different taste for the new millennium. There were few people who were very interested up to quite recently, but it seems to be changing. Watch this space!'

TULLAMORE DEW

The roll-call of distilleries and brands which disappeared when the Irish industry imploded is an extensive one. Locke's Kilbeggan (now revived under Cooley), Dundalk, Allman's Bandon, Comber and Tullamore are just some of the famous and respected distillers who simply found it impossible to carry on, no matter how good people thought their whiskey was. Most of the brands simply disappeared, the names of the distillers and their whiskeys slowly slipping into a vaguely remembered past. Some, however, managed to hang on. Tullamore Dew is one of them. It also represents a history of the Irish industry in miniature.

ABOVE *Daniel E. Williams put the Dew into Tullamore Dew.*

BELOW *Cantrell & Cochrane have opened a heritage centre on the site of the old distillery.*

The Tullamore distillery was built in 1829 and was bequeathed to the Daly family in 1857. In 1887, Captain Daly – a man more interested in playing polo, hunting and racing horses – made Daniel E. Williams manager. Williams was a bit like an Irish Jack Daniel, having joined the plant at age 15 and speedily worked his way up to this lofty position. The fact that a country gentleman like Captain Daly was involved in making country whiskey is evidence of how wealthy landowners began to take over from farmer-distillers as the rural population declined and new laws were passed.

Williams expanded the distillery, began exporting and created a new triple distilled pot still brand, Tullamore Dew (the 'Dew' taken from his initials) which was sold with the slogan 'Give Every man His Dew'. The quality of his 8-year-old whiskey even moved that normally crusty old historian Alfred Barnard to poetry. Eventually the Daly family sold their shares to the Williams', but popular though it was, even they couldn't keep the distillery running. In 1954, the Tullamore distillery closed.

It was a tough time for Irish whiskey. The government had, for reasons best know to itself, restricted exports of whiskey during the Second World War arguing that it would ensure ready supplies on the domestic market and continue to bring in guaranteed revenue. The UK government, on the other hand, had decided that while the whiskey industry was

run down, some distilleries could stay open and exports should continue. It was a monumental blunder by the Irish. The distillers, meanwhile, were still holding firm to their belief that traditional pot still

LEFT *A fine and very different 12-year-old from Tullamore Dew.*

whiskey was superior to blended Scotch.

When the government raised taxes again in 1952 the writing was on the wall for distillers like the Williams' of Tullamore. No way could the domestic market support so many brands. The Irish may be famous drinkers, but even that was beyond them. In 1953 a survey by the Irish Export Board discovered that 50 per cent of whiskey-drinkers in the States had never heard of Irish whiskey. Irish emigrants now saw themselves as Americans, they had turned their backs on the 'ould country'.

Thankfully, Tullamore Dew was saved when the business was sold to Power's in 1965 and the next year became part of the Irish Distillers portfolio. These days it is owned by Cantrell & Cochrane, though the whiskey is still made at Midleton. A classic blend of traditional pot still with light grain, it's in the lighter end of the spectrum, though a 12-year-old version shows considerably more weight – probably from a higher percentage of pot still. The overall lightness has endeared it to German and, more recently, American palates. People are interested in the brand once more and Cantrell & Cochrane has opened a heritage centre at the old Tullamore distillery site. All positive enough, but you can't help but wonder, what if …

TASTING NOTES

Tullamore Dew

On the lighter side of the Irish fence. Clean crisp and light, but not hugely exciting. **

Tullamore Dew 12-year-old

So different from the standard bottling that you wonder initially if it is from the same stable. Ripe, fleshy and rich, this is the one to try. ***(*)

COOLEY

KILBEGGAN○LOCKE'S○MILLARS○ TYRCONNELL○CONNEMARA

Ever since Bushmills joined Irish Distillers in 1973, one firm made all the Irish whiskey in the world. When, in 1989, a group of businessmen announced that they were starting a rival firm, Cooley, a few people's ears pricked up. Surely Irish Distillers would welcome some honest competition – after all, two firms selling the story of Irish whiskey to the world must be better than one. But the tale of Cooley has as many twists and turns as a story by Flann O'Brien. After Cooley was up and running, Irish Distillers launched

a bid for the new firm, stating that once it was brought into the group they would close it down.

The Cooley board – strapped for cash – had actually accepted this fait accomplis before the Irish government's competition authority leapt in, declaring the move would contravene monopoly regulations. Cooley, much to its surprise, was given a stay of execution.

It was still tough going financially. It's not easy setting up a whiskey distillery. For starters, you have to lay down stock and then sit on it for at least three years before you can even sell your first bottle. Add in the costs of plant, barrels etc., and you are looking at a

KILBEGGAN *The original name of the Locke's distillery in County Westmeath, founded in 1757. John Locke bought the plant in the 1840s and expanded steadily until the disastrous 1920s struck. Kilbeggan stumbled on before finally giving up the ghost in 1953. Cooley now ages its whiskey in the old warehouses and has converted the site into a museum.*

TASTING NOTES

Kilbeggan
Very clean and faintly grassy, with a touch of camphor on the nose. Sweet and gentle, with grass and nuts playing off each other. ✳✳

Locke's
Broader and riper than Kilbeggan, showing a sweeter, fruitier palate. Pretty young, with a crisp and peppery finish. ✳✳

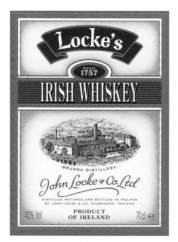

huge investment – particularly in a world market which really wasn't that bothered about Irish whiskey. If Irish Distillers couldn't persuade the world to drink brands other than Jameson, what chance would this whippersnapper have?

Then Cooley signed a deal with Heaven Hill in Kentucky, who started selling the young whiskies in the US and things began to look that little bit brighter. Now the situation is much more stable. Cooley's brands are available across Europe and America, it has diversified into supermarket private label and is making whiskey for a number of other firms, such as Hennessy. What's even better for the whiskey lover is that the Cooley brands offer a different perspective on what Irish whiskey tastes like. There's no unmalted barley in its brands, no

triple distillation either – they've even released a peated malt.

It's another element in Irish whiskey's revival. 'We started distilling on Easter Sunday 1989,' says their ever-enthusiastic distiller David Hynes, 'and without wishing

MILLARS *Originally an old Dublin whiskey made for one of that city's wine and spirit merchants.*

TASTING NOTES

Millars
Fragrant and peachy. Well rounded with good malty, sherried notes. A deliciously juicy little number, with an oomph of fruit to finish with. ✳✳✳

LEFT *The beautiful Locke's distillery, a victim of the Irish whiskey crash, but now home to Cooley's museum.*

COOLEY
KILBEGGAN ○ LOCKE'S ○ MILLARS ○
TYRCONNELL ○ CONNEMARA

Tyrconnel now is made up of whiskeys ranging from five to 10 year of age giving it greater weight and substance on the palate. The wood mix has been fixed as well – with the majority of the malts being aged in vanilla-rich first-fill ex-Bourbon barrels, with the balance being aged in second- and now third-fill casks. 'The wood has to be balanced,' says David. 'If you are planning on releasing a 25-year-old malt, you'll want to put it in a butt or a second fill barrel, otherwise you'll be chewing on trees'.

Locke's shows more distinct wood influence and occupies a slightly richer, fruitier perch – mainly due to the higher percentage of eight- and nine-year-old whiskies used in the vatting, but the real surprise for most drinkers is the peated Connemara. Although its peating level is lower than Highland Park or Talisker, the smoke still comes stomping out of the glass, mingling with the naturally-sweet malt. An acquired taste for people brought up on 'traditional' Irish whiskey – and one which David himself had to pick up. 'When I tasted my first Islay whisky, I thought it was awful!' he admits. 'But you've got to persevere with these things. The idea of a peated malt in Ireland was a new one and the first reaction here was the same as mine when I tried the Islay, but we've broken through now'.

He's now trying to acquire a taste for sherried malts, though he confesses he hasn't quite got to grips with Macallan ... yet. 'Sherry casks are something we'll be looking at for the malts,' he says. 'So are fresh casks ... there's nothing to stop us using some of them either'.

The malts may be the main weapon in the Cooley armoury, but the firm is capable of producing some pretty smart blends as well. The grain whiskey is from maize: 'it gives us the sweeter taste that we're looking for,'

to be accused of blasphemy, you can say the resurrection of the Irish whiskey industry started that day'.

It certainly offered a dramatic alternative to the gospel according to Irish Distillers, which stated that all Irish whiskey should be triple distilled, unpeated and have unmalted barley in the mashbill. 'It's traditional malt distilling,' says David, 'though while the principles are much the same as in Scotland – pot stills, malted barley and double distillation – our spirit still has cooling tubes in its lie pipe which partially condense the vapour and redirect it back into the body of the still, giving it a higher than average rectification'. In other words, it makes it lighter.

Whereas Irish Distillers builds its profile around Jameson, Cooley has decided to concentrate its efforts on promoting its three-strong range of malts, Tyrconnel, Locke's and Connemara, with the main focus being put behind highly drinkable Tyrconnel. If you haven't tried it for a while you'll be in for a surprise. Cooley, after all, can now draw from a greater range of ages of malts, and while the column still, similar to those at Girvan and Invergordon, is in David's words: 'a pretty smart piece of equipment which allows us to play a lot of tunes'.

He goes on: 'We want to leave a lot of flavour in our grain whiskey. You don't want a bland flavour when you're blending. All you'll do then is dilute the malt. One of the most distinctive things about our blends is their malty nose. After all, when you drink a blend, or any whiskey, you want development in the mouth. It should be like music, with different notes coming through as it goes through the palate; a whiskey that's the same at the start and the finish is a boring whiskey.'

Sensibly enough, Cooley has steered away from battling it out with Irish Distillers on their ground. It made more commercial sense to offer an alternative rather than a replica. 'You can't take on a big brand like Jameson head-on,' says David. 'We had to do something different. There was no point in us gearing ourselves up to sell a million cases of a brand from the word go, we wouldn't have had the money. We had to gear up and say 'how can we get into that market, where's the niche?' Malt was it'.

Cooley's arrival has been a major contributory factor in Irish whiskey's renaissance – whereas at the start of the 1990s you would be lucky to find more than two or three Irish brands on the shelf, now there's a whole raft of new products, not just from the new kid on the block but from Irish Distillers as well – and Cooley is now sound financially. 'We're out of our infancy,' says David. 'There may have been doubts over our ability to survive in the past, but no longer'.

The fact that the firm has come so far so quickly is not just the result of some clever positioning on the market, but speaks volumes about the increasingly high quality of their whiskeys – and there's plenty more to come as the existing stock continues to mature. After all, the only way you can tell how your whiskey is going to look at 18 years of age is by sticking it in a cask and waiting. There will be plenty more new ideas coming out of County Louth in the future, you can bet on that.

TASTING NOTES

Tyrconnel Single Malt
Young and lively, with a pleasant clover/cut grass nose and a touch of sulphur. Sweet, biscuity and light, with a lemon-pie kick and cereal on the finish. Young and clean. ✳✳(✳)

Locke's Single Malt
Delicate and fresh, with some rounded apricot yoghurt/custard notes. Ripe on the palate, with a malty finish mixing grass and juicy fruit. Attractive. ✳✳✳

Connemara Single Malt
Attractive turfy peat smoke aroma, with some germoline/band aid and floral perfume behind. Seems to split on the palate, with the smoke going one way and the fruit the other, but like all the Cooley brands its getting better and better as the malts get older. ✳✳✳

AMERICAN WHISKEY

For Scottish and Irish settlers in the mid-1700s, the first sight of Kentucky must have seemed like a promise of paradise. This wasn't the wet, hard-boned lands of their birth, but a fertile place with fast-running water, stands of white oak and abundant wildlife. Their joy was confirmed by a guarantee of 400 acres of free land if they were willing to clear the land and plant Indian corn (maize). They had brought their pot stills with them, so the corn could be turned into whiskey: here were small farmers doing what their ancestors had long done, and here was the birth of the American whiskey industry.

By the 1780s, commercial distillers such as Evan Williams and Jacob Beam were up and running, shipping their wares downriver to New Orleans in barrels branded 'Bourbon County'. Soon, whiskey had become so popular that, by the mid-19th century, the Temperance movement had swung into action. By the start of the 20th century, temperance had hardened into abstinence and by 1915 Kentucky and Tennessee were dry. Prohibition (1920–33) devastated the industry: the public may have drunk more liquor than before, but it was imported spirits, not American whiskey. On Repeal, a small band of brave distillers started up again,

only to be shut down again during World War Two. By the time the bourbon industry was operational again, Scotch had taken over.

It has been tough going until relatively recently, when the trend to 'drink less but better' and a renewed appreciation of classic cocktails, like the peerless Manhattan, prompted the release of new premium bourbon brands. Maybe the 21st century will bring more joy than the last.

So what gives bourbon its character? As ever, a combination of ingredients: the calcium-rich water, the mix of grains, the distillation and the method of ageing. Each distiller then composes his own variations on the basic theme. By law, the mashbill must contain a minimum of 51 per cent corn, though most distillers use around 70 per cent. The rest consists of 'small grains': malted barley, wheat or rye. Some only have one mashbill, others use different ones for different brands, or even for the same brand. After cooking, the mash is pumped into the fermenter, where yeast and backset are added. Each distillery will have its own jealously-guarded strain of yeast, which it claims is a major contributor to the character of the whiskey.

The mash must also contain a minimum of 25 per cent backset, the spent liquid left at the foot of the beer still after the first distillation. (High in acidity, it helps to balance the pH in the ferment.) All American whiskey is made by this 'sour mashing' process.

The first distillation takes place in a column still (the beer still), although the methods used for the second distillation vary. Some condense all the vapour and then redistil it in a pot still called a doubler; some run the vapour straight through the doubler, while others use a 'thumper' – where the vapour passes through a vessel filled with water. Only Labrot & Graham uses pot stills.

The new spirit is then put in new charred barrels for a minimum of four years. A few distillers mature their whiskey in warehouses that are heated in winter, but the majority age in wooden rack warehouses up to 10 storeys high. Since heat rises, the higher up you go the hotter it gets, thereby giving the whiskey in the upper floors a different character to that ageing at the bottom. To get a consistent product, distillers will either blend a cross-section of barrels or laboriously rotate those at the top with those at the bottom. The barrels chosen as single barrels or small batch releases tend to come from the middle floors.

All this – the rich new make spirit, its sweet corn base mingling with the subtle jabs of rye or soft silky wheat, the sweet vanilla, honey and spice of the new wood – combines to make bourbon one of the world's great whiskey styles.

Note:
Proof refers to American data about alcohol content; 100% proof is 50%ABV.

JIM BEAM

Jim Beam is one of the big names of bourbon, so there's no surprise to find a big man behind it all. Booker Noe isn't just physically huge, he is one of the foundation stones of the modern industry. Booker is Jim's grandson and still lives in Jim's old house in Bardstown. Talk to him and you are tapping straight into the history of bourbon itself.

Today, Jim Beam is the world's biggest selling bourbon, but in 1934 things weren't so rosy. Prohibition had been in force for 13 years, and there was no stock left. To start up again would be expensive and risky. But this didn't deter Jim who, aged 70, built a new distillery in Clermont in just 120 days. What else could a Beam do? Whiskey making runs in their veins. After all, Booker's great-great-great grandfather Jacob Beam started making whiskey commercially in 1795. 'This was the distilling capital of the world before it was put out of business by the government,' says Booker. 'Why did he start it up again? Remember, he'd been in the whiskey business for 40 years before Prohibition. Beams have now been making bourbon for 205 years.'

Booker has now passed the reins to Jerry Dalton, the first non-Beam to be appointed master distiller. The fact that he lived in the house directly behind Booker's is pure

coincidence. 'Well, even a blind hog finds an acorn every so often!' he laughs. For all his modesty, Jerry is a highly respected distiller and, though reluctant to give away too many company secrets, will take you deep into the process.

There's a sequence of special quirks at work in Beam's two plants, but it's yeast that Jerry zooms in on. For Scottish distillers, yeast is merely a catalyst that converts sugar to alcohol and CO_2. However, for bourbon distillers it has almost mystical properties and each firm guards its own strain(s): Beam is still using the yeasts propagated by Jim in his kitchen in the 1930s.

'Different yeasts produce different levels of fusel oil, which will ultimately have an effect on the flavour,' Jerry explains. 'In ageing, the fusel oils form esters with whatever acids are present. Each yeast will give different proportions of these fusel oils, so you get different flavour profiles.' When you combine the special yeasts with the

BELOW *The old homestead at the Jim Beam distillery.*

LEFT *Jim Beam who, at age 70, rebuilt his distillery and started all over again.*

Prohibition they cut the proof or blended it to make it go further. Now flavour's coming back. The industry's been badly beat up, but now it's rolling again. It'll be back now that people are tasting this super-good whiskey. Hell yes, bourbon's back.'

higher-than-average percentage of backset (which produces what Jerry calls Beam's 'bold' flavour), and the two-and-a-half times distillation (the vapour from the beer still passes through a thumper before being redistilled in the doubler) the signature Beam character is taking shape.

But if Jim Beam White Label is the world's best-known bourbon, it's the firm's small batch range which is rightly making waves. The four-strong selection is clear evidence of how complex a spirit bourbon can be, but the one closest to Booker's heart, not surprisingly, is the one which he selects personally and which carries his name. 'Booker's is the only one that's bottled at the same proof at which it went into the barrel,' he says, with considerable relish. 'It's whiskey like it was a hundred years ago'.

If the style hasn't changed, the methods certainly have. Does today's high-tech approach of distilling make Jerry less of an artist and more of a scientist? 'I'm a bit of both,' he says. 'There's an art to making bourbon that has evolved over two hundred years, but I'm also a scientist who wants to find better ways to control the process and preserve the mystery behind it all'.

The techniques may be space-age, but the small batch range signals a return to a time when bourbon meant big, bold and flavoursome whiskey. 'People just kinda got away from flavour,' muses Booker. 'After

TASTING NOTES

Jim Beam White Label 4-year-old 80°proof
Lightly oaked, with some light spicy notes. Clean and sound. ✲ ✲

Small batch range

Basil Hayden 8-year-old 80°proof
Light and rye-accented, with plenty of lemon and tobacco leaf notes. Clean, with crisp rye mixing it with dark, ripe, nutty fruit. ✲ ✲ ✲

Baker's 7-year-old 107°proof
Richer, with a leather armchair kind of nose and lots of overripe fruit. Slightly biscuity to start with, then good sweet vanilla fruit. ✲ ✲ ✲

Knob Creek 9-year-old 100°proof
Rich and sweet with honey, blackberry and spun sugar. Elegant and super-ripe, with a hint of vanilla and some light cinnamon spice on the finish. ✲ ✲ ✲ ✲

Booker's 7-year-old 126.5°proof
Amazingly complex without water, for such a powerful Bourbon – and a bit like a grizzly bear dancing. Huge and flavour-packed with raisin, chestnut honey, black cherry, pepper, cinnamon and toffee. Rich and immensely powerful, mixing orange peel, crème brûlée and tobacco/cigar blown along by a hickory wind. Immense. ✲ ✲ ✲ ✲ ✲

WILD TURKEY

One of the more intriguing aspects of bourbon's revival is the way in which its stubborn old guardians have been proved right. None more so than Wild Turkey's Jimmy Russell. A glance at the Wild Turkey distillery confirms that this place doesn't abide by convention. As other firms are tidying up their plants, the iron-clad, black-painted Wild Turkey sits teetering on the brink of a gorge, steam rattling out of various chimneys. It is one of those places which feels alive, as if the plant is humming with the measured rhythm of the staff. And, overseeing it all, is the avuncular Jimmy.

Take a walk with Jimmy through his distillery – it may be owned by Pernod-Ricard, but this is Jimmy's place – and it comes alive. The swirl and changing colours of the ferment; the wheeze, hiss and whistle of the still – these are not inanimate functions, but part and parcel of a creative, living process.

No surprise, then, that he's a firm believer in the human touch. 'People are one of the most important things in making bourbon,' he says. 'It's people who are doing the work here, people with generations of experience. All these proud people feel that Wild Turkey is part of them'.

He talks of understanding the meaning in the weird music of the still. 'You have to have a stillman there, watching and listening to it. The sound tells him what is going on. We can hear a funny noise and know what's happening. You can't have that hands-on control with machines'.

Jimmy is no technocrat. His pride in his distillery and his whiskey springs from the heart. 'There are things which you cannot prove scientifically. You can't prove why copper works better than stainless steel, but you sure can taste the difference. So, for me, making whiskey is a craftsman's process, an artistic process if you like. That artistic element is coming back as bourbon's image improves, and small batch and single barrel brands appear. People are coming back to an old-fashioned way of making whiskey and old-fashioned flavours'.

BELOW *An unconventional site for an off-the-wall whiskey.*

BELOW *Jimmy Russell,
the genius who is
behind the mighty
Wild Turkey.*

Superb though they are, it's Wild Turkey 101° proof, 8-year-old which defines top-end bourbon. Uncompromising yet charming (like Jimmy himself), the fact that Hunter S. Thompson rates it as his favourite bourbon is no surprise, and speaks volumes about what to expect.

This belief in flavour is a crucial factor in making Jimmy's the tastiest bourbon of all. 'Old-fashioned' is often used in a derogatory sense, but when distillers such as Jimmy Russell use the term, they're talking of a style of bourbon made before the 'light is right' brigade began to throttle the industry to death. These days, people like him have been vindicated, as the whisky-drinking world (re)discovers flavour and complexity. 'They wanted us to go lighter and lighter, but we never did change,' he smiles. 'You'll see more and more flavoursome, top-end bourbons in the future: but we didn't have to change anything, we were already there!'

Everything in the production of Wild Turkey is done to maximize flavour. The mashbill is heavy on rye and barley malt, it's distilled to a lower proof than any other bourbon and aged for longer than average. Jimmy also insists on using 'the old, natural ageing process', by rotating the barrels in the warehouses – taking the barrels from the hot top floors and replacing them with those that have started on the cool lower floors. It gives a more even maturation profile for the Wild Turkey brands, though it's the middle floors which provide the whiskeys that go into the small batch Rare Breed and single barrel Kentucky Spirit.

TASTING NOTES

Wild Turkey 80° proof
Big nose, mixing geranium orange peel and dark fruit. Some smoke on the palate, which is rich with light cinnamon/perfumed notes, then a crisp vanilla/toasty finish. Solid stuff. ✳✳✳

Wild Turkey 8-year-old 101° proof
Wonderfully rich and complex nose of acacia honey, caramelized fruits/crème brûlée, faded roses and dried spices. Starts sweetly then sits heavily in the mouth. Hugely rich, mixing tingling sweet spices, honeyed fruits, vanilla and some red fruit. Succulent, and a meal in a glass. ✳✳✳✳✳

Wild Turkey Rare Breed 108.6° proof
Slightly sweeter than the 8-year-old 101°: more barley sugar/candy notes. Big and honeyed, with a light floral lift. Lovely mix of roses, fragrant spice, plum, nectarine and cigar box. A slow, soft start in the mouth, then a lift of charred wood, honeyed wood and a mix of chocolate and lemon on the finish. ✳✳✳✳(✳)

MAKER'S MARK

The Samuels, like the Beams, are part and parcel of Kentucky's history. The family has been a distillers since 1780, and their TW Samuels brand was an early classic. One of their ancestors, Rueben Samuels, married Zerelda James, whose sons became better known for a less peaceful way of life. Bill Samuels, current boss of Maker's Mark, still has Jesse's and Frank's pistols hanging on the wall of his office.

A discussion of the human influence on whiskey leads Bill to muse on his father, Bill Samuels Sr, who was something of a visionary in these parts. He bought the run-down Happy Hollow distillery in 1953 and started making a new kind of bourbon his way, in a different, softer style. After consulting another legend of the industry, Pappy Van Winkle, he created a new mashbill using winter wheat instead of rye, aged the whiskey for longer and sold it at a higher price. Not the standard approach in post-war Kentucky.

'In 1953, Dad was talking of how people were looking for a more refined version of bourbon,' recalls Bill. 'He knew the things that he wanted to preserve, the ones he wanted to throw out. He was going to create a bourbon to suit his taste: it had damn-all to do with the market! He just thought bourbon should taste better'. The industry is full of such purely personal likes and dislikes dictating the taste of a brand. Bill Sr simply didn't like aggressive whiskey, so he changed everything.

His was a gentle crusade. The family may be related to the James gang, but coming out guns blazing just ain't their style. Bill Sr may have had the vision, but it was his son who took Maker's Mark across the world, talking up high-quality, premium-priced liquor at the time the industry was at its nadir. Still, the Maker's Mark crusade must have seemed doomed. 'In the 1960s there wasn't a nickel's-worth of difference between bourbon and bourbon-flavoured vodka', says Bill.

RIGHT *Every bottle of Maker's Mark is hand-dipped in wax.*

'The industry was at the end of the road because no-one could afford the $100 barrel. Bourbon can never be a mass-market commodity, because we have that high cost legally built in'. Having to buy new barrels is less problematic when the product is selling for a higher price.

You can list the differences in production that set Maker's Mark apart: the mashbill; the yeast strain created by Bill's great-great-grandfather; the double distillation; the charcoal added to the white dog as a filtering agent; the air-dried wood; the way the barrels are rotated in the high-rack warehouses. All these give the product its character, but ultimately Maker's Mark is about the stubborn Samuels family and the people who work in the distillery.

Bill Sr has been proved right. These days premium bourbon is one of the most exciting areas in world whisky, but Bill refuses to take the credit for this turnaround. Like all great whisky men he realizes he's part of a team. 'If

TASTING NOTES

Maker's Mark 90°proof
Lovely, complex mix of flowers, cumin, cinnamon, marzipan/anise, vanilla and light honey. A soft start, then great interplay between silky-soft honeyed fruit, vanilla-toffee and balanced oak flavours. Some chocolate on the finish. Gentle, easy and complex. *****

I could do one little thing, I'd bring out my ancestors to see that bourbon is finally no longer a wilderness product. The six generations before me did the heavy lifting,' he says. 'Dad said he'd change the face of bourbon. When he started no-one gave him a chance, but by the time I retire bourbon will be the talk of the town'.

He believes the new premium sector will be a major factor in restoring pride to the industry. 'Higher margins fire up the creative juices,' he says. 'The industry is improving and the products are infinitely better, because they are high price. Now there's an opportunity for the talented people in the industry to practise their art and not just produce a low-cost product. The question is whether we have sufficient discipline not to disappoint people's high expectations … that's what Dad would have said.'

ABOVE *Half-empty, or half-full? Maker's has brought back a new confidence to the bourbon industry.*

LEFT *Maker's Mark remains the most charming distillery in Kentucky*

FOUR ROSES

Driving up to Seagram's Four Roses distillery makes you feel strangely like Warren Oates at the start of *Bring Me the Head of Alfredo Garcia*. This bizarre lemon-coloured confection of a Mexican-style ranch seems incongruous with Kentucky's gentle rolling grasslands and tree-lined hollows. Thankfully, master distiller Jim Rutlege is more hospitable than the patriarch in Sam Peckinpah's violent film classic.

This is the last remaining Kentucky outpost of the mighty Seagram empire: in fact, until the firm's Lawrenceburg plant in Indiana reopened it was the only Seagram distillery in the United States – stark evidence of the decline that beset the American whiskey market from the 1970s.

That hasn't stopped Jim making a pretty classy whiskey at Four Roses, with 'pretty'

being the operative word. It's a given that every distiller has his or her own technique, but Four Roses stands apart from its colleagues in Kentucky. Perhaps it is Seagram's Canadian roots showing through, but no other distillery in the state makes such a range of different base whiskies. With five yeast strains being used on the two mashbills-one with 75 per cent corn, the other with only 60 per cent-Jim has 10 subtly different whiskies to blend into the Four Roses style. When you drop in different distilling strengths and different ages you've got a pretty complex package of flavours.

'We feel that you get most of the flavour from the small grains,' says Jim. 'In our case that means rye and some malted barley.' He then explains that, contrary to popular belief, bourbon-makers don't use malted barley solely for its enzymes, but for flavour and another little-known property. 'Malt does two things,' he says. 'There's the enzyme conversion which begins to break down starch molecules and change them into soluble and therefore fermentable, sugars, and also liquefies the corn slurry by breaking down its molecular structure'.

Jim therefore adds malted barley twice during cooking (mashing). First, the corn is cooked at a high temperature with some malt, to help liquefy the thick gloop; then the temperature is dropped and rye is added (this stops rye balls forming and cuts down the risk of bacterial infection in the ferment). Then the temperature is reduced once more and the malted barley (along with some backset) is added for its enzyme.

The mention of backset triggers a long and patient explanation about pH levels, consistency and soleras. 'The backset comes from the bottom of the still and is high in acidity,' says Jim. 'It is put into the cooker and the fermenters to get the correct pH. As the ferment proceeds, the pH drops and turns sour. You know by the smell and taste how far it is advanced. It is science and art combined'.

Jim places a priority on careful monitoring of the process, from smelling the grains as they arrive, right through to the end

TASTING NOTES

Four Roses Yellow Label
Gentle and lightly oaked, with fragrant lemon notes. A great mixer. ✳✳✳

Black Label
Firmer and smokier, with hickory wood, honey and a crisp rye-accented finish. ✳✳✳(✳)

of the distillation – and on to maturation. 'I'm looking for a rich, sweet aroma from the new spirit,' he says. 'But to do that you need to have built-in good flavours to begin with, and they are first generated in the ferment. You can run a still wrong, but you can't make your basic material any better'. Even the maturation is different here; in a single storey palletized warehouse, rather than the traditional racks. But, hey, who is to say what is right and what's wrong? The end results – the precise, pretty, spicy Yellow Label and the richer, complex Black Label – are bourbons of the first order.

LABROT & GRAHAM

When Brown-Forman, owner of Jack Daniel's and the imposing Early Times plant in Louisville, announced in 1994 that it had bought the derelict Labrot & Graham distillery in the heart of prime bluegrass horse-rearing country, some people thought it was branching into bloodstock. When the company declared it was making triple-distilled, pot-still bourbons at its new plant, there were plenty of others muttering into their Manhattans. Some $8 million later, the distillery is up and running, its whiskey is maturing nicely in the stone-walled warehouses and tourists are flocking to see this glorious renaissance of a genuine old-time Kentucky distillery.

It was appropriate that Brown-Forman should choose this site as the home of its new premium small batch brand, Woodford

Reserve, as this distillery is no stranger to innovations. As the Old Oscar Pepper distillery it was here in the 1830s that Scotsman James Crow started and perfected the sour-mashing process, tested for acid and sugar levels, used hydrometers and studied the science of ageing – effectively creating what we know as bourbon.

But why bother with a new distillery when you already have a perfectly good site making the defiantly old-fashioned, wood-panelled Old Forester? Let L&G's general manager Bill Creason explain. 'We had developed a super-premium [now Woodford Reserve] in Louisville, but when we examined other categories we realized the importance they put on the actual place it was distilled. So, we realized we should have another distillery operation for these new products'.

But why use pot stills when the rest of the industry uses columns? 'It's the way it would have been made in the old days. We talked to people in Scotland about the differences you get with pot stills and found that people didn't move to column stills because they made better whisky, but because they made it more cost-efficiently'.

So, armed with three stills made by Forsyth's of Rothes and expert advice from

BELOW *That was then ...*

LEFT *... This is now.*

TASTING NOTES

Woodford Reserve
Gorgeously silky mix of bitter orange, honey, smoky wood and a hint of mint. Beautifully balanced between sweet vanilla/honey fruit and grippy wood. Long and utterly charming. ✳✳✳✳✳

Ed Dodson (see page 24), Brown-Forman's Lincoln Henderson and Dave Scheurich began to get their heads round the intricacies of pot still distillation, which took time. 'You have to get used to the subtleties of any new piece of equipment,' says Bill. 'We just worked at it. We got to know the process, when to cut, how to heat and the quality just got better and better'.

Now both Woodford Reserve and the, as yet unnamed, 'super-premium' bourbon are maturing in L&G's heated stone warehouses. You may raise an eyebrow over such an apparently authentic old-style distillery having heating, but Bill is quick to respond. 'We went back to the old records and found that the oldest warehouse we use was being heated as early as 1892. With two and a half foot thick stone walls, even in a Kentucky summer it wouldn't be warm enough inside to age the whiskey properly'.

The relatively high proof off the still, the low barrel proof, the heated warehouses and the fact that the barrels also have charred heads combine to make Woodford Reserve one of the most honey-rich, complex bourbons on the market. What can we expect from the new boy? Well, the mashbill uses four (rather than the usual three) grains, having both wheat and rye, but we'll just have to wait for a couple of years. 'These aren't bourbons to mix with Coca-Cola,' says Bill. 'They are to be enjoyed like a single malt'.

There are further parallels with Scotland in the approach L&G has taken to visitors, and a few ideas, such as a 'smellometer', borrowed from wineries in the Napa Valley. For Bill, this is an education centre for American whiskey. 'This is the oldest operational distillery in America,' he explains. 'Whiskey has been made on this site since the mid-1700s. It's not as far back as Scotch, but, heck, it's as far back as we can go in America! We're trying to educate people about that, about bourbon itself, as well as ourselves. We've let the Scots take centre stage, now it's our turn'.

BUFFALO TRACE

You only need to cruise down 7th Street in Louisville to see how big the American whiskey industry once was. What were once distilleries and warehouses are now massive brick mausoleums. Weeds have cracked through the concrete, pool parlours and strip joints line the littered sidewalks. These abandoned sites are silent relics of a time when distillers thought the world was ready for their whiskey.

There's another, strangely little known behemoth of a place in Frankfort, but thankfully its prospects are much rosier. A beautiful redbrick distillery in a hollow next to the Kentucky River, it's a place where whiskey has been made commercially since the 1860s. It used to be known as OFC Distillery, George T. Stagg, Schenley, Ancient Age and Leestown. It's now called Buffalo Trace, after research revealed it sits on a path or 'trace' used by buffalo on their way to cross the river. The change of name has brought a new visibility and a greater willingness to engage with people, while the plant's $6 million renovation has called time on the barbed wire fences. 'The pride factor has increased with all the changes,' enthuses brand director Chris McCrory. 'Not just the people working here, but the folk in Frankfort too'.

LEFT *Buffalo Trace was strategically built next to the river, handy for getting its whiskey to market quickly.*

BELOW *Whiskery whiskey-making the old way.*

Whether you taste Ancient Age, Blanton's or the new eponymous brand, you cannot fail to notice the mix of honey-sweet fruitiness in the distillery's whiskeys. It could be down to the mashbill, or the high percentage of backset used; but for Chris, the Buffalo Trace signature comes from the tight wood management and the skill of its master distillers. 'We have the highest reject rate in the industry' says Chris, 'and are working to very tight parameters; from the char down to what part of the tree and even what side of the mountain it should be from'.

Unusually, the warehouses are heated in winter. 'You get a stop-start style of maturation in racks,' explains Chris. 'This is a more fluid process which, I believe, gives us a better product.' So, instead of having rapid maturation during the hot summer and no movement in the winter, the fact that the warehouses are kept at a fairly constant

ABOVE *Founder Colonel Blanton keeps a watchful eye on things.*

temperature keeps the whiskey moving in and out of the wood.

This tight wood policy and the fact that the warehouses range from five to twelve floor wooden racks, to giant three-storey units has allowed Buffalo Trace a wide scope in blending. Because barrels on different levels mature at different rates (and therefore give diverse styles) a product such as Ancient Age can be cross-blended between warehouses and floors, while the sweetest barrels from the prime spots can be isolated and bottled as single barrels. 'Ancient Age and Blanton's have the same mashbill,' explains Chris. 'But while Ancient Age is mingled from 300 barrels from different levels, Blanton's is one barrel-usually from the middle section of the same warehouse. We're looking at how we make our products and how, without changing existing practises, we can experiment with different flavours and styles'.

Now that Old Charter and the wheated W.L. Weller have been added to the portfolio, Buffalo Trace is becoming a major player in the new-look bourbon industry. Weller is a particularly appropriate addition, as this was Pappy Van Winkle's brand, the man who kept a sign outside his office that read: 'No chemists allowed. This is a distillery, not a whiskey factory.' It fits in with Chris' belief that the human touch makes the difference between a good bourbon and a great one. 'We're the only distillery that doesn't have a computer running the stillhouse,' he claims, with evident pride. 'For us, bourbon is more of an art than a science. The human element is there all the time'.

TASTING NOTES

Ancient Ancient Age 10-year-old 86° proof
Spicy menthol nose: some marzipan, beeswax, vanilla custard and a hint of clove. Clean, fruity palate of tangerine, apple, lemon and a nice vanilla crunch on the finish. ✳✳✳(✳)

Buffalo Trace 90° proof
A rich mix of cocoa butter, cedar wood, honey, chocolate and hickory smoke. Soft palate, the wood showing a little, with a rounded mocha/cigar box finish. ✳✳✳(✳)

Eagle Rare 10-year-old 50.5° proof
Plush, spicy nose with vanilla and some honey. Soft and sweet with light cocoa, honey and black fruits. A rich, rounded treat. ✳✳✳✳

W.L. Weller 7-year-old 90° proof
Fragrant nose of fresh herbs, berry fruits, some tar, caramelized orange/marmalade, tanned leather and cinnamon. Soft and mellow in the mouth, mixing vanilla, coffee and cream. Fragrantly beautiful. ✳✳✳✳✳

Old Charter 8-year-old 80° proof
On the leaner side, with some white pepper, orange/lemon peel and light oak. Easy palate, mixing almost oily honeyed fruit and a crack of rye. ✳✳✳

Benchmark 8-year-old 80° proof
Incredibly fragrant nose, like warm hot cross buns. Dry and slightly dusty palate, with crisp wood. ✳✳

Blanton's Single Barrel 93° proof
Sweet – almost syrupy – nose, with cedar, cocoa, vanilla and plum and lifted clove/lemon notes. Raisins in a cigar box. The palate has ripe dark fruits with some chocolate, underpinned by chewy honeyed fruit. In the precise, well-balanced distillery style. ✳✳✳✳(✳)

HEAVEN HILL

Kentucky's weather has a fair impact on bourbon. The extremes of summer and winter temperature affect its maturation; twisters occasionally slam into warehouses, reducing them to matchwood; and electrical storms can, in Heaven Hill's case, destroy a distillery. On 7 November 1996 a lightning strike ignited a warehouse, sending barrels of

blazing whiskey exploding into the air and, like some hellish game of dominoes, triggered fires in neighbouring warehouses. Eventually a river of flaming whiskey detonated the distillery, leaving it a freakish mess of twisted, mangled metal.

An absent distillery and the ongoing demands of multiple brands would drive

TASTING NOTES

Evan Williams 7-year-old 90°proof
Graceful. Spicy wood, cinnamon, caramel and a little smoke on the nose. The palate has mixed roast nut, leather and some tobacco leaf, with a fine bite mid-palate. ✳✳✳✳(✳)

Elijah Craig 12-year-old 94°proof
Rich, with balanced woody notes, spice, smoke and some nutmeg. Chewy, fruity palate and great length. ✳✳✳✳

Elijah Craig 18-year-old
Almost heathery nose, with some saddle soap/leather and rich nuttiness. Soft, rich fruit on the palate and a balancing spicy pepperiness. Excellent. ✳✳✳✳✳

Evan Williams Single Barrel 1989 86.6°proof
A leafy nose, with a nice balance between lemon leaf, dry nut, white pepper, varnish, cedar wood, herbs, honey and a touch of sesame oil. Soft yet fresh. ✳✳✳✳

LEFT *Heaven Hill believe in a hands-on approach to whiskey making and are keen to promote human involvement.*

many people to the wall, but Heaven Hill is made of stern stuff. For three years the firm produced its extensive range in the Early Times distillery, before buying UDV's Bernheim site in Louisville in 1999. For Heaven Hill's master distiller Parker Beam, it was a chance to work in his own plant again, though he first had to get to grips with Bernheim's idiosyncrasies.

'Every plant has its own characteristics,' he says. 'There were some kinks here which we had to iron out before we could get the Heaven Hill character right. We've been in there, banging on pipes and bringing it round to our way of working'. While UDV built Bernheim as the most technologically-advanced distillery in America, Parker has begun to re-introduce human involvement to the process. 'Though it is highly automated, we've always worked in a more hands-on fashion. That's where the art of making whiskey comes in and it's something that we'll always hang on to'.

'Art' is a word he uses frequently. The son of a master distiller, whiskey making runs through his veins. For Parker, 'art' means less automation and a belief in skill and experience. Staying true to the Heaven Hill style is paramount and that, as he says, means keeping control of a number of small things 'which make this whiskey better than the average bear'. For example, he insists on using only one mashbill for the main Heaven Hill brands, such as Elijah Craig and Evan Williams. 'The advantage of this is that every

drop has to be top quality, because you never know if it is going to end up in a main brand, a small batch or a single barrel'.

The fact that Heaven Hill has superb brands at 12-, 18- and even 23-years-old reinforces his argument against the myth that bourbon does not improve in barrel after six years. In fact, he argues, Heaven Hill brands don't start to blossom until they are at least seven years old. Why, then, is this misconception so widely peddled? 'A lot is down to the fact that it's the victors who write the history' he says, with a certain irony. 'Because the biggest bourbon brands aren't aged for a long time, that was the myth put about. It makes economic sense to release a whiskey when it's young: we do, but our flagship [Evan Williams Black Label] is seven years old'.

It's a further example of the new confidence coursing through the industry. Master distillers such as Parker are now encouraged to display the full range of their skills, from standard brands to the small batch and single barrel brands, which he describes as 'the purest manifestation of the master distiller's art'.

With a vast portfolio encompassing standard brands, single barrel, extra aged, vintage and now the ex-UDV brand Old Fitzgerald, Heaven Hill is well placed to make an assault on world markets. 'Our quality standards have never varied,' says Parker. 'I guess I just don't know how to do it any other way'.

BARTON

Barton's distillery is a no-frills kind of place. While other firms are finding ways to attract tourists, Barton goes about its business with none of the flummery that sometimes surrounds whiskey making. It's a solid, blue-collar distillery that wouldn't seem out of place in *The Deer Hunter*.

That down-to-earth aspect surfaces when you talk to Barton's master distiller Bill Friel. 'The public's perception of Jim Beam is totally related to Booker Noe,' he reasons. 'A lot of firms don't have that luxury, so they have to rely on what they do internally.' Don't let that fool you into thinking that Barton makes cheap-end whiskey. Bill and Ken Pierce, Barton's chief chemists, are as obsessive about quality as any other distiller. 'My job is about making a superior product' says Bill, 'and making it so it's identifiable as a Barton whiskey'.

A 'Barton whiskey' means a brand with an unashamed catch at the back of the palate. 'Some folks call it a bite,' says Bill, 'I prefer to call it a sharpness. It's not to the detriment of the whiskey, it is a quality that appeals to people.' Bill feels that sharpness comes from the still: the top part of the beer column has a full set of copper plates and the vapour is condensed before it goes into the doubler. 'The art of whiskey making is about how you control the still,' he says. 'Here it's the way the upper part is constructed to allow reflux and how we control the temperature at the head to remove volatiles.'

When you toss in the different mashbills for the wide range of Barton brands, you're looking at a complex range of flavours from one site. Bill and Ken remain modest about their skills. The fact that Barton bought brands from UDV doesn't faze them. 'We don't play about with distillation techniques,' says Bill. 'We've a variety of mashbills, so we can make rye or corn styles successfully. If I have to modify the still I can, so it's not impossible to replicate a product at a different distillery. What's important is to maintain the integrity of the brand'.

Bourbon has been made on this site since 1889 and Bill has little time for many of the new ideas gaining currency in today's industry. Don't expect to find heating in the Barton warehouses either. 'The only reason people are doing that is to shorten the ageing cycle and allow them to sell it sooner. In my

TASTING NOTES

Ten High 80° proof

Assertive nose, with plenty of dry spice (nutmeg/cinnamon) and some lemon notes. Whipcracks into the mouth, with light caramel fruit and a zap of high-toned rye on the finish. Uncomplicated but fine. ✵✵

Very Old Barton 6-year-old 80° proof
A charred, slightly sooty nose with some Olde English marmalade notes. That sootiness is on the palate as well, followed by a short sharp shock of rye on the finish. ✵✵✵

ABOVE *A no-frills kinda place. While others take the tourist route, Barton gets on with whiskey making.*

RIGHT *It may look industrial, but there is artistry at work.*

mind if you're doing that you're making whiskey, not bourbon.' Neither has Barton entered the single barrel or small batch market. 'We didn't see it as profitable, or something which would last' says Bill. 'We'd have to have created a new brand, which would detract from Very Old Barton and we would have set aside selected barrels which were significantly better. I know where the honey barrels are, but we already use 'em!'

Bill's one of the generation of distillers who guided bourbon through some pretty torrid times and isn't too keen on what he sees now that things are easier. 'I've got no problem with making a profit,' he says, 'but the whole world is in a rush to squeeze every

penny of profit out of a business as quickly as possible.' For him, tradition isn't some prettified past, but an issue of integrity and individuality. 'Tradition and proven standards are essential for continuing the success of any product. It doesn't take long to ruin a brand,' he says with conviction. Now the acid test is getting the Kool-Aid generation (as Bill describes them) away from vodka to the honest Barton style. 'It's easier than it has been,' he says with a grin. 'But the middle-aged yuppies were brought up on pop drinks, so there's a little problem to convince them that's it's a bit more sophisticated to sit with a glass of good bourbon and water in front of you than a glass of Coor's!'

JACK DANIEL'S

The Jack Daniel's legend starts with the eponymous founder of the distillery, who allegedly owned his first distillery at the tender age of 13, having learned his skill at the knee of Dan Call – one of those moonshining preachers who pepper the history of American whiskey. Jack was a clever operator, but it's hard to imagine that he envisaged his brand would one day become the most famous American whiskey of all.

These days it's Jimmy Bradford who wearing Jack's shoes. The epitome of a Southern gentleman (unlike the short-tempered Jack, who died after kicking a safe in his office), he's been looking after the whiskey for 32 years, which, he drawls laconically: 'probably gives me some credibility to talk about distilling'.

They make whiskey slightly differently in Tennessee, though it's not – as many people think – sour-mashing that sets it apart. All Bourbon and Tennessee whiskey is made by the sour mash technique: the real difference lies in the Lincoln County Process, or charcoal mellowing, which all Tennessee whiskey must undergo.

For Jimmy, it's the combination of the limestone water drawn from Cave Spring and the mellowing that helps to give Jack Daniel's its personality. The mellowing involves dripping the new spirit though a 10-foot vat of maple charcoal, which leaches some fusel oils and esters from the spirit, while giving it a distinct softness.

There's only one mashbill – 80 per cent corn, 12 per cent rye and 8 per cent barley malt – for all the Jack Daniel's brands; meaning that the sole difference between such diverse products as Green Label, Black Label and Gentleman Jack lies in the length of time they have been aged and where they have been warehoused. With a spread of traditional warehouses, the blenders can mingle whiskeys from different sites and floors to make up the desired product, and with 7,500 barrels a week being put into the warehouses, they have plenty of choice.

That figure gives an idea of the sheer scale of the operation. Owner Brown-Forman

ABOVE *The founder.*
A whiskey-maker at 13,
progenitor of one of the
world's best-known
brands.

may, rightly, play up the Sleepy Hollow-type imagery surrounding the small town of Lynchburg, but don't be fooled: this is a bang-up-to-date distillery applying old techniques in a highly efficient and modern manner. Jack may recognize the site, but he'd be astounded by the three huge beer stills and intrigued by the way in which the vapour is fed directly into the doubler, making it a refined type of single distillation.

But you don't think of Jack Daniel's in production terms. The visitors who pour into the distillery aren't that interested in mellowing, distillation techniques or the pros and cons of mechanization. They come because they feel part of a family. When an Australian winemaker I know went to America for the first time, the two places at the top of her 'must-see' list were Graceland and the Jack Daniel's distillery. It's that kind of loyalty that makes Jack an American icon.

These days, Jack Daniel's is as recognizable a symbol of American rock 'n' roll rebelliousness as Harley Davidson. It hasn't gone out and developed a bad-boy image, but clutching one of those square bottles with the black label brings out the rebel in even the most mild-mannered accountant, and makes him feel, if only for one drink, the equal of Keith Richards or Dennis Hopper.

You would think that being in charge of such an iconic product would prey on Jimmy's mind, but there's no chance of that. He approaches this onerous responsibility with the same pleasant, measured good humour as he does the rest of life. 'It's a pleasure to assist in making this product. Just to drive in every day and see Jack standing there down the holler gives me a sense of pride'.

TASTING NOTES

Jack Daniel's Black Label 80°proof
Very sweet and clean, with a touch of licorice, smoke and caramel. A good mouthful with a great, sweet finish. ✳✳

Gentleman Jack 80°proof
Even sweeter, with black fruit and a sooty, rich finish. ✳✳

RIGHT AND BELOW
Despite being the rock 'n' roll brand par excellence, Jack *still portrays itself as a 'Sleeply Hollow' kind of brand.*

ONCE OUR TENNESSEE WHISKEY gets inside the barrel, it isn't in much of a hurry. And neither are our barrelmen.

Loading a truck with full barrels is hard labor. So you can't blame Richard McGee, Clay Fanning and Tim Thomas if they're in no rush to get to the barrelhouse at the top of the hill. Because that's where this batch of Jack Daniel's will age for years until it's sippin' smooth. If it doesn't get up the hill right away, no one will mind. Least of all, the folks who will enjoy what's in these barrels years from now.

SMOOTH SIPPIN'
TENNESSEE WHISKEY

THE ONLY REASON Jack Daniel settled in our hollow was this cool limestone cave spring.

In 1866, folks said Jack Daniel wasn't good at business. He built his distillery twelve miles from the nearest railroad. But Mr. Jack was a whiskeyman first, a businessman second. So he settled alongside this spring of pure, ironfree water. One sip, we believe, will tell you why we still use this water. (And why Jack Daniel wasn't so bad at business after all.)

SMOOTH SIPPIN'
TENNESSEE WHISKEY
Your friends at Jack Daniel's remind you to drink responsibly

Tennessee Whiskey • 40-43% alcohol by volume (80-86 proof) • Distilled and Bottled by
Jack Daniel Distillery, Lem Motlow, Proprietor, Route 1, Lynchburg (Pop. 361), Tennessee 37352 • www.jackdaniels.com
Placed in the National Register of Historic Places by the United States Government

Tennessee Whiskey • 40-43% alcohol by volume (80-86 proof) • Distilled and Bottled by
Jack Daniel Distillery, Lem Motlow, Proprietor, Route 1, Lynchburg (Pop. 361), Tennessee 37352
Placed in the National Register of Historic Places by the United States Government

DICKEL

Tennessee has another distillery which, for some unaccountable reason, tends to be overlooked when people talk of American whiskey. Indeed, you wonder if Dickel's parent company, UDV, has forgotten about it as well; until you remember that UDV sold off its major Kentucky distillery and brands, but kept this little place. Perhaps they recognized the sheer quality of the spirit produced by master distiller Dave Backus.

Dickel is a place which – even in the down-home, slow-talking world of American whiskey – is the most laid-back, the most relaxed on the block. It is also small in an industry where consolidation has resulted in bigger and bigger plants producing large volumes. Inevitably you end up comparing Dickel with Jack Daniel, but in truth the differences are significant. For Dave Backus they all stem from the fact that Dickel's size has allowed it to retain a means of making whiskey that large plants simply cannot justify.

'We'll only produce 1,500 bushels a day,' he says. 'The big guy down the road makes around 12,000. We're small, we're not highly automated, we have people here who have been making whiskey for 20 or 30 years, guys who know what to look for'. Dickel, for Dave, represents that marriage of experience and skill, and he remains a craftsman more in tune with his senses than with any fancy instrumentation.

'The guy taking in the grains has unloaded truck after truck in his career. Now, corn may seem all the same to you, but it ain't, so you rely on that guy's experience. When you're highly automated you don't know there's something wrong until you've distilled it. Seeing or smelling something that might not be right is the biggest advantage of being small and having people around; it becomes almost instinctive'.

The more you dig the more the differences appear. Take the charcoal for the mellowing vats. Dave's specifications are strict: only buying the sugar maple when the sap is down, to eliminate the chances of bitter, green components in the wood. Bigger producers, he argues, have to buy wood all year round.

The mellowing process is slightly different, too. Rather than dripping it in, Dickel uses a flooded chamber, allowing

BELOW *Tennessee's secret distillery, at one time the largest in the state, now its best-kept secret ... but not for much longer.*

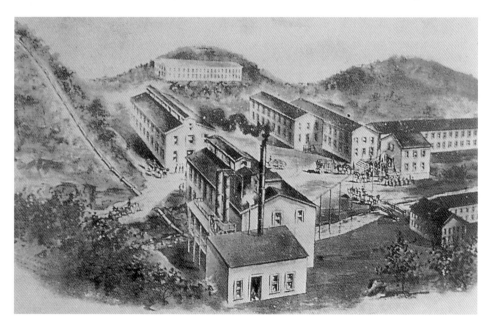

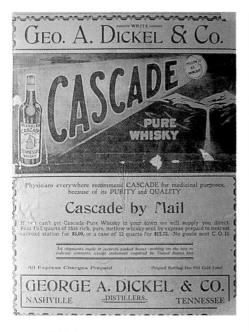

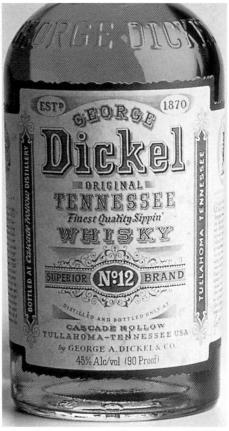

ABOVE *Dickel's Cascade whiskey was one of the first to take advantage of mail-order sales.*

greater contact between the white dog and the wood. The first distillation is fully condensed before running through the doubler. The mashbill is high in corn, with rye and malted barley making up the small grain component. All have a part to play.

The warehousing is also different. Dickel uses single storey houses that are heated in the winter. 'Multi-storey racks age differently from top to bottom,' Dave explains. 'In a single storey warehouse, the barrels are only six high and you have no need for rotation, while the air ventilation controls the temperature and evens out the ageing cycles.' Dave feels this is why Dickel can age for a relatively long time, with no evidence of over-woodiness.

He's a distiller who immerses himself in the production of his spirit, but fears passion like his is on the way out. 'I think that skills will disappear,' he broods. 'You don't know how to make whiskey if all you're doing is programming a computer. Whiskey changes every day and the only way you can know

TASTING NOTES

George Dickel No.12 90°proof
Lightly honeyed, with a little touch of cedar and some basil and mint. Lovely length. Stylish. ****

George Dickel Special Barrel Reserve 90°proof
A good unctuous nose, with sweet butterscotch/caramel notes. Cinnamon, nutmeg and cumin on the palate, with ripe fresh fruit – apple, orange and tangerine. Sexy. *****

what to do and how to do it, is with experience.' His complex, refined whiskey proves his point. Sadly, Dickel remains almost unknown and UDV seems intent on keeping it that way. Dave won't be drawn on that one. 'I just make it and drink it' he says.

The Scots may argue that their whisky is the world's most popular style because of its inherent quality, but a quick exploration of whisky's convoluted history soon shows that Scotch was boosted by a sequence of fortuitous historical circumstances: phylloxera, Prohibition, Irish independence and World War Two all combined to clear the playing field. What if the Irish Question had been resolved peacefully? What if Prohibition hadn't lasted as long?

Playing that game helps to fuel long nights of debate, and raises many more questions; such as why hasn't Canadian whisky become Scotch's main international rival? It was closer to America during Prohibition and it boomed post-war, as America went 'light'. The problem was that the Canadian industry had set its sights at the easy-drinking, mass market. When the international whisky slump took hold in the late 1970s, Canada was caught cold. Now there are as many distilleries in the whole of Canada as there are in Kentucky.

But this doesn't exactly explain what makes Canadian whisky special. Historically it started off in much the same way as the American industry, with rye whiskies made

CANADIAN WHISKY

by emigrant crofters from Ireland and Scotland. As the pioneers began heading into the interior they started making spirits from whatever came to hand. As ever, the landscape dictated the style and the psyche, so when these early distillers reached the gentle, fertile lands around the Great Lakes and the verge of the vast prairies they began to make a gentle, soft style of whisky.

Inevitably, these small-scale producers gave way to larger firms – particularly when the Coffey still made it across the Atlantic in the mid-19th century, and when the Canadian government decided that spirits were a soft target for large tax levies. Only the big boys making large volumes from continuous stills could survive.

The government was so keen to control the whisky industry that by the turn of the 20th century, Canadian whisky was governed by the toughest regulations in the world. The Canadians flirted with Prohibition in 1918, but were fortuitous in that just as they abandoned the experiment America went dry. The distillers on the Great Lakes were in seventh heaven and some made their fortunes by selling their (legally produced) whisky to besuited, Fedora-wearing American customers. It proved the making of Hiram Walker (now part of Allied Domecq) and Sam Bronfman's Seagram, the two firms which still dominate the industry.

The major Canadian players thought differently to their Scottish counterparts.

Rather than having a large number of small plants making unique whiskies, they consolidated production and developed means of distilling which enabled a vast range of whiskies to be made on a single site. Now, the major brands all have a large percentage of high-strength, corn-based whisky at their core, to which has been added a number of flavouring whiskies. These can be made from a wide selection of mashbills, distilled to different strengths and aged in a variety of woods. Then, distillers are permitted to add up to 9.09 per cent of other imported mature spirits (or wines) to the blend: brandy, malt, rum, sherry and bourbon are all used. Delicate they may be, but lacking in flavour? Never.

This integration of modern technology meant that when the international downturn arrived, the major names simply consolidated their distilleries. Seagram demolished three sites, including Sam's beloved La Salle plant in Montréal, and now makes all its whisky at Gimli in Manitoba. Hiram Walker shut down its British Columbian outpost in Okanagan and Gooderham & Worts in Toronto, and now only uses Walkerville in Ontario. Only the small, innovative Kittling Ridge and Glenora have bucked this trend.

But, just as the world wakes up to quality whisky, the Canadians politely settle down in the background. It's not in their nature to push their gentle, delicate whiskies at international consumers, but it's our loss.

CANADIAN CLUB

Understanding Canadian whisky and, in this case, Canadian Club means getting acquainted with a significantly different style of whisky. For Canadian Club's affable master blender Mike Booth, it all revolves around a deep understanding of 'lightness'. 'You can't make bourbon light,' he says, 'it has to be distilled to a low proof. It uses a heavy mashbill and has to be aged in new casks. In Canada, the intention is to produce a light, easy-to-drink product – but not a simple one'.

This is where the art of the Canadian whisky maker comes to the fore, not least because the Canadian industry – though tightly regulated – allows considerable scope for innovation. Canadian producers can distil to any strength: for example, Canadian Club's grain whisky component is rectified to just under 95% ABV. 'It doesn't have a "grainy" character,' says Mike. 'It's close to vodka that has been aged in wood for six years'. The brand is based on a combination of this grain whisky and the critical flavouring whiskies. These rye, rye malt and barley malt whiskies are each distilled to different strengths – one in a copper column, another in a combination of column and pot still, the third a combination of different distillates. The link is the intense, zesty, lemon-tinged flavour of rye.

Most Canadian Club is then pre-blended and aged, although some of the flavouring

TASTING NOTES

Canadian Club
Delicate, with a crisp and lightly smoky nose. There's a hint of rye and a soft, easy palate. A good all-rounder. * * *

Canadian Club 12-year-old
Gentle, with cream toffee notes. A ripe, soft start with lots of vanilla/custard and a ripe maltiness. The palate is silky-smooth, like chocolate-chip ice cream, with a bite of rye on the end. * * * *(*)

whiskies are kept aside and aged separately. Lightness is still the key and in the standard six-year-old maybe only 15–20 per cent of the flavouring whiskies are blended in. Nor is there a heavy wood influence, for as well as using only ex-bourbon barrels, refills are extensively used – as are recharred barrels. 'We're using barrels that have been used six or seven times,' says Mike. 'Recharring is another element of control. A light whisky will have a low percentage of rechar; a heavier one will have more; while the flavouring whiskies are all in 100 per cent

LEFT *Hiram Walker, godfather of Canadian whisky.*

the public face of his beloved Canadian Club.

Not surprisingly, he believes that this seriously undervalued brand is the whisky the world is calling out for. A cocktail aficionado, his evangelical zeal has converted some pretty influential barmen. 'Canadian Club has an advantage over other whiskies in cocktails, because it works well as a blending ingredient – it doesn't overpower. It's also a great hot-weather whisky: who wants a heavy whisky when the sun's beating down?'

We're back to the vexed question of light again. 'People think light means dilute, but it means delicate,' he says. 'Think of it this way: Canadian Club is like a light tea, while bourbon is stewed tea. It's lots of tannins against very few'.

Light is just one of the problems that quality Canadian whisky has to counter. 'The majority of producers haven't wanted to talk it up,' Mike argues. 'It's a wonderful story; a romantic, exciting story. Most people think of Canadian whisky as boring, but they'd find it much more interesting if they knew what went into it'.

rechar. It's a pretty good system'. This flexibility (plus the 9.09 per cent) allows Canadian Club to be made in a number of different guises. The standard 6-year-old has no additions, while the 10-year-old has an addition of separately aged flavouring whiskies and brandy.

Mike's own CV parallels the convoluted complexities of the Canadian industry. He helped build the Okanagan distillery in British Columbia, the idea being to make Canadian Club three thousand miles away from its home in Walkerville, Ontario. 'We got it close,' he admits, 'but it was never quite right'. He was soon overseeing another project at Okanagan; this time building a malt distillery to produce bulk malt for Japan. Sadly, both plants are now mothballed, but Mike keeps going, now as

BELOW *Things may have changed, but Canadian Club has always insisted on high quality.*

SEAGRAM

The advantage of having such flexible regulations is that Canadian distillers can draw on a huge number of different methods to assemble a brand. Inevitably, this means that each firm has its own secret ingredient. For Seagram, the core of their flagship brands – VO and Crown Royal – is a grain whisky that has been made by a batch process in a single column. 'Although it is distilled to 94%ABV, we take off the heads and the tails as well,' explains master blender Art Peterson. 'The result is a more flavoursome distillate than the standard Canadian grain'.

The flavouring whiskies are equally complex. They include a powerful straight rye; a 'bourbon' style and two barley whiskies – an 'Irish' style from unmalted and malted barley and a 'barley bourbon'. It doesn't end there. Different yeasts are used, not just for the different mashbills but sometimes for the same one, to give subtle variations on a theme. 'You can create a whisky with high fusel oils with one yeast,' explains Art. 'Another will give a "bourbon" style with estery notes, another gives floral notes'.

Some of these flavouring whiskies are made in Canada's only Coffey still. In the 1930s, Sam Bronfman avidly studied how the DCL Scotch blends were created and realized that Coffey still grain was fundamental to their style. Sam's influence remains strong. 'The fact that we make more blending whiskies than many of our competitors was inherited from him,' says Art. 'His aim was to present the blenders with as many

TASTING NOTES

Seagram's VO
An aromatic, delicate nose leading into a soft yet complex palate, with some lemon, sweetcorn, malty notes and mature pulpy fruit. ✳✳✳(✳)

Crown Royal
More succulent, with lots of light spice and creamy toffee fruit. Elegant and gentle, yet mouthfilling. ✳✳✳✳✳

RIGHT *The royal jewel in Seagram's crown, the brand is one of Canada's best and most complex whiskies.*

different types of whiskies as possible'. A blend such as VO or Crown Royal will have 35 different types of whisky, including bourbon and rye from Indiana.

Unlike other distillers, Seagram doesn't pre-blend. 'You can achieve a great deal by working in separate lots,' says Art. 'It all makes commercial sense: if you're working with a portfolio of blends, you have the ability to blend some away if you have an excess. You can't do that if you've pre-blended, because there's no flexibility'.

Different barrel types-first-fill ex-bourbon, refills and new wood-are matched to different whiskies. 'Each time it's refilled, the barrel changes,' explains Art. 'You get fewer wood extractives, while the different maturates also give a different character. For example, if you refill a barrel with grain when it has previously held rye, you'll get some of the rye quality in the grain'.

It gives Art and his team a wide range of building blocks with which to construct the personality of the delicate VO and succulent Crown Royal. Though the mashbills and yeast(s) are similar in both brands, each has a different percentage of rye or 'bourbon' flavouring whiskies, as well as different ratios of batch grain and Coffey. Though the wood recipes are different as well (more of Crown Royal's flavouring whiskies are aged in new wood to increase the coconut/vanilla notes), Art believes the secret is the percentage of batch grain used. 'It masks the woodiness of whiskies aged in new wood. Crown Royal without batch grain would be noticeably woody'.

The remarkable thing is that Seagram produces this array of whiskies on one site. For Art, this isn't just the triumph of technology, but a demonstration of human skill. He has been a distiller in two plants as well as a blender and now oversees quality control for all Seagram's North American plants. 'That has led me to appreciate how many people are involved in the process,' says Art. 'As master blender I approve every blend, but it takes a lot of people to make it. Each brand has its own team, then behind them there's the people who buy the grain, distil the whiskies and look after the wood. You have to have people'.

KITTLING RIDGE

Just as you've got accustomed to the sheer scale of distilleries in Canada – there may not be many, but they make up for their lack of numbers by sheer size – you come across Kittling Ridge and its two small pot stills. It's as far away from the big guys as you can imagine. Based in Grimsby, Ontario, it's the brainchild of John Hall who, after spending 20 years making Canadian wine, decided to try his hand at making spirits as well.

In 1992 the Kittling Ridge distillery opened up, taking Canadian whisky in a new direction. John isn't that concerned about the power of the multinationals: he calmly gets on with things, making new converts and trying out new techniques of making Canadian whisky. And hey, who said there was only one correct way? The rules, after all, are loose enough to allow an enterprising producer enormous scope for experimentation.

John may be serious about quality, but he doesn't take life too seriously. 'All the big guys can say they are 12th-generation whisky makers: well, I'm a first generation whisky maker – and the first New World whisky maker. OK, I may have started the race a hundred years late, but I'm small, I'm independent and I'm trying to create something new and unique'.

But hang on a minute, this is Canada, a country which has witnessed a radical shrinking of its industry. If the big guys can't

do it, what kind of a crazy man decides to start making whisky just as everyone else is closing down distilleries? 'People certainly thought I was crazy in 1992,' laughs John, 'but now I'm employing 120 people, the whisky is number one in Taiwan and sales are growing at 25 per cent a year in Canada'.

So, what is he doing that's so different? 'Rather than replicate, I've tried to develop unique whiskies. I'm not imitating anyone else, I'm making a hand-crafted whisky with its own fingerprint. A lot of the big guys are doing what they did a hundred years ago, but I'm trying to do something new'.

The main difference lies in the exclusive use of pot stills and a clever variation on the Canadian theme of making a range of different flavouring whiskies. At Kittling Ridge there are three: one rye, one corn and one malted barley, each of which is distilled separately and then aged separately in American oak, with three different charring

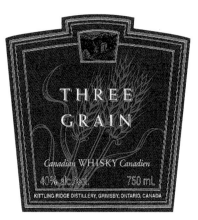

TASTING NOTES

Kittling Ridge

Forty Creek Three Grain
*Light amber in colour, this one needs dilution to reveal a vibrant mix of light honey, dry spices, vanilla, sandalwoood and lemon zest. Soft and smooth on the palate before a good zap of rye on the finish. A whisky (and distilery) to watch.
***(*)*

Forty Creek Barrel Select
Mellow and soft on the nose with silky toffee/vanilla notes combined with plump rainined fruit and dry spiciness. The flavour is softer and more chewy than the 3 Grain with a mix of prune and custard. ***(*)

LEFT *A Brave New World for whisky. Kittling Ridge's cutting-edge new releases.*

BELOW *John Hall, winemaker turned whisky man.*

levels – from light toast to heavy char. With his new 40 Creek Barrel Select, John has gone one stage further. 'I wanted to try sherry mellowing, but didn't have any sherry butts. So I used my winemaking knowledge and made some sherry, kept it in the barrels for three years, then sold the sherry and rounded off the whiskies in the barrels!'

He's now thinking of releasing the three flavouring whiskies as limited edition 'single varietal' whiskies, evidence that there's still something of the free-spirited New World winemaker in his approach. 'As a winemaker I was trying to create nuances by ferment, yeast, ageing and grape varieties,' he says. 'Whisky's exactly the same: there's the same craftsmanship, the same subtleties – the impact of different chars on the barrels, distillation cut points and grain types instead of grape varieties'.

John believes that 'New World' whisky is about flavour, about taking chances, about exposing the public to new ideas. 'Canadian whisky has been sold as a mild-tasting

whisky to be mixed with soda pop, but I believe the consumer's palate is more sophisticated these days. This is my attempt to bring back craftsmanship and creativity, and show them that exciting flavours can be discovered if whisky is made with sensitivity'.

VISITING

Whisky tourism is now big business and most distilleries are open to visitors. Most tours will include an audio-visual display, a guided walk round the distillery and a free dram (not applicable in the US because of licensing laws). The cost of entry is normally redeemable against a bottle from the shop. Please remember that all distilleries have a 'silent season' at some point during the year, in order to carry out essential maintenance work. It is always best to telephone to double-check times of opening, especially if you are with a large group.

SCOTLAND
Highland Park, Kirkwall, Orkney
Tel: 01856 874619
www.highlandpark.co.uk
Open April to October, 10am–5pm;
July to September, Mon–Fri 10am–5pm, Sat-
Sun noon–5pm
Tours every half hour, last tour 4pm
November to March, tours 2pm only; shop
open 1pm–5pm, Mon to Fri
Closed Dec 24th to Jan 5th (open
Hogmanay)
Shop, coffee shop

Pulteney, Huddart Street, Wick, Caithness
KW1 5BD
Tel: 01955 602 371
www.inverhouse.com
Tours by appointment only

Clynelish, Brora,
Sutherland KW9 6LR
Tel: 01408 623000
Open March to
October, Mon–Fri
9.30am–4.30pm;
November to
February, Tues–Thurs
9.30am–4pm, or by
appointment
Shop

Glenmorangie, Tain, Ross-shire IV19 1PZ
Tel: 01862 892477
www.glenmorangie.com
Open all year, Mon–Fri 9am–5pm
June to August, Saturdays 10am–4pm
Sundays noon–4pm
Closed Christmas holiday period
Tours from 10.30am. Last full tour 3.30pm,
or by appointment
Maximum 15 per group, pre-booking
advisable
Visitor centre, museum, gift shop

Balblair Distillery, Edderton, Tain,
Ross-Shire IV19 1LB
Tel: 01862 821273
www.inverhouse.com
Visits by appointment only

Glen Ord, Muir of Ord, Ross-shire IV6 7UJ
Tel: 01463 872008
www.glenord.com

Open March to October, Mon–Fri
9.30am–5pm;
July to September, Sat 9.30am–5pm; Sun
12.30–5pm. Last full tour 4.15pm
November–February, restricted opening
hours. Please telephone
Closed Christmas and New Year
Shop, exhibition

Glen Moray, Bruceland Road, Elgin
IV30 1YE
Tel: 01343 542577
www.glenmoray.com
Open all year, Mon–Fri 9am–5pm
Closed Christmas holiday period
Tours at 9.30am, 10.30am, 11.30am, 2pm,
3pm, 4pm, or by appointment. Maximum 10
per group
Visitor centre, shop

Longmorn/Benriach
Not open to the public

Glen Grant
Tel: 01542 783318
Rothes, AB38 7BS
Open mid-March to October, Mon–Sat
10am–4pm; Sun 12.30pm–4pm
June to September, closes one hour later
Visitor centre, shop, extensive Victorian
gardens

Glenrothes
Not open to the public

Strathisla, Seafield
Ave, Keith AB55 5BS
Tel: 01542 783044
www.chivas.com
Open February to
November, Mon–Sat,
9.30am–4pm; Sun
12.30pm–4pm
Closed weekends
February to mid-
March
Shop, tutored tasting,
self-guided tour

Speyburn Distillery, Rothes, Morayshire
AB38 7AG
Tel: 01340 831 213
www.inverhouse.com
Visits by appointment only

Mortlach
Tel: 01313 377373
Not open to the public

Balvenie
Tel: 01340 820000
Not open to the public
www.thebalvenie.com

Glenfiddich, Dufftown, AB55 4DH
Tel: 01340 820373
www.glenfiddich.com
Open all year (excluding Christmas and New Year) Mon–Fri 9.30am–4.30pm,
Easter–October, Sat 9.30am–4.30pm; Sun noon–4.30pm
Admission free
Shop, museum, cafe
Advance booking essential for coach parties and groups of over 12

Macallan, Easter Elchies House,
Craigellachie AB38 9RX
Tel: 01340 871471
www.themacallan.com
Open telephone for appointment
Admission free
Shop

Aberlour, Charlestown of Aberlour,
Banffshire AB3 9PJ
www.aberlour.com
Generally not open to the public other than on special open days. Phone for details

Cardhu, Knockando, Banffshire AB38 7RY
Tel: 01340 872555
Open, March to November, Mon–Fri 9.30am–4.30pm;
December to February, Mon–Fri, 10am–4pm
July to September, Sat 9.30am–4.30pm, Sun 11am–4pm
Malt whisky shop, exhibition

Tamdhu
Not open to the public

Knockando
Not open to the public

Glenfarclas
Ballindalloch AB37 9BD
Tel: 01807 500257
www.glenfarclas.com

Open April to September, Mon–Fri 9.30am–5pm; Sat 10am–4pm;
June to September, Sun 12.30–4pm
October to March, Mon–Fri 10am–4pm

Cragganmore, Ballindalloch, Banffshire AB37 9AB
Tel: 01807 500202
Not open to the public.
Tours, by appointment, are only available to members of Friends of the Classic Malts.
For details contact Friends of the Classic Malts, PO Box 87, Glasgow G14 0JF

Glenlivet
Ballindalloch, Banffshire AB
Tel: 01542 783220
www.theglenlivet.com
Open mid-March to October, Mon–Sat, 10am–4pm; Sun 12.30–4pm;
July to August open until 6pm daily
Café, museum

Ardmore
Not open to the public

Glen Garioch
Not open to the public

Royal Lochnagar, Crathie, Ballater, Aberdeenshire AB35 5TB
Tel: 01339 742716
Open Easter to October, 10am–5pm. Tours from 10.30am–4pm
In winter months phone for availability
Distillery closed at weekend
Small groups only. Shop stocks entire UDV malts range, including a complete selection of rare malts

Dalwhinnie, Dalwhinnie, Inverness-shire
PH19 1AB
Tel: 01540 672219
Open: March to December, Mon–Fri
9.30am–4.30pm; June to October including
Sat 9.30–4.30pm;
July & August including Sun 12.30–4.30pm
Last tour one hour before closing
Restricted hours between December and
March; telephone for times
Closed between Christmas and New Year.
Exhibition and shop

Edradour
Moulin, by Pitlochry, Perthshire
Tel: 01796 472095
www.edradour.co.uk
Open: March to November, Mon–Sat
9.30am–5.00pm; Sun noon–5.00pm;
November to mid-December, Mon–Sat
10am–4pm
Admission free

Glenturret, Crieff, Perthshire PH7 4HA
Tel: 01764 656565
www.glenturret.com
Open February to December, Mon–Sat
9.30am–6.00pm (last tour 4.30pm); Sundays
from noon.
January is 'Silent season', free tours Monday
to Friday 11.30am–4.00pm (last tour
2.30pm)
Closed 25th/26th Dec and 1st/2nd Jan
Adults £3.50, Children £2.30, under 12s free
VIP Tour (includes extensive free tasting)
Connoisseurs' Tour (includes tasting of rare
vintages)
Restaurants, cafe, bar, museum, shop,
conference facilities (with ISDN link)

Glengoyne, Old Killearn, Dumgoyne,
Stirlingshire
Tel: 01360 550254
www.glengoyne.com
Shop, museum

Oban, Stafford St, Oban, Argyll PA34 5NH
Tel: 01631 572004
Open all year, Mon–Fri 9.30am–5pm; Easter
to October Sat 9.30am–5pm; July to
September, Mon to Fri 9.30am–8.30pm
Last tour one hour before closing
Restricted hours operate from December to
February
Closed Christmas Day and New Year period.
Exhibition, shop and museum

Ben Nevis
Tel: 01397 702476
Lochybridge, Fort William
Tours all year Mon–Fri 9am–5pm; plus
Easter to October, Sat 10am–4pm
July to August 9am–7.30pm Mon–Fri
Shop, video

Talisker, Carbost, Isle of Skye IV47 8SR
Tel: 01478 640314
Open April to June, Mon–Fri 9am–4.30pm;
July to September, Mon–Sat 9am–4.30pm;
October, Mon–Fri 9am–4.30pm;
November to March, Mon–Fri, 2–4.30pm
Last full tour 4pm
Exhibition and shop

Jura
Craighouse, Isle of Jura, Argyll
Tel: 01496 820240
Tours by prior arrangement only

Bunnahabhain, Port Askaig, Islay, Argyll
Tel: 01496 840646
www.bunnahabhain.com
Open March to October, 10.30am, 1.30pm,
2.45pm; November to February , telephone
to arrange a suitable time
Admission free
Shop and free tasting

Bowmore Distillery, Bowmore, Islay, Argyll
PA43 7JS
Tel: 01496 810441
www.morrisonbowmore.com
Open all year
Tours Mon–Fri 10.30am, 11.30am, 2pm,
3pm (summer only); Sat 10.30am (summer
only)
Rest of year Mon–Fri 10.30am and 2pm
Shop, tasting bar, all walkways ramped for
wheelchairs

Laphroaig
Tel: 01496 302418
www.laphroaig.com

Lagavulin, Port Ellen, Islay, Argyll
PA42 7DZ
Tel: 01496 302730
Open all year, Mon–Fri
Please phone for appointment

Ardbeg, Port Ellen, Islay, Argyll PA42 7EA
Tel: 01496 302244
www.ardbeg.com
Open all year Mon–Fri 10am–4pm
June to August, Mon–Sun 10am–5pm
Tours from 10.30am, last full tour 3.30pm or
by appointment
Maximum 10 per group, pre-booking
advisable for larger groups
Admission redeemable against shop purchase
Visitor centre, gift shop and restaurant
(opening hours as above)

Springbank
Tel: 01586 552085
Open to visitors May–Sep, Mon–Thurs
Tours at 2pm, prior notice needed
Admission redeemable against shop purchase

Fettercairn Distillery,
Fettercairn, Laurencekirk, Kincardineshire
AB30 1YB
Tel: 01561 340205
fettdist@jimbeam.co.uk
Open May to September, 10am–5pm (last

tour 4pm)
Admission free, booking advised for coach
parties
Shop

Auchentoshan
Not open to the public

Glenkinchie, Pencaitland, Nr Tranent, East
Lothian EH34 5ET
Tel: 01875 342004
Open all year, Mon–Fri 9.30am–5pm, last
tour 4pm
Easter, Bank Holiday Weekends and
weekends from 5 June to 31 October Sat
9.30am–5pm, Sun noon–5pm
Last tour 4pm
Closed Christmas Day, Boxing Day
Exhibition, shop and whisky bar

ALSO RECOMMENDED
Speyside Cooperage, Dufftown Road,
Craigellachie AB38 9RS
Tel: 01340 871108
Open all year, Mon–Fri 9.30am–4.30pm;
June to September, Sat 9.30am–4.30pm
Last tour Fri & Sat 4pm
Café, shop

Scotch Whisky Heritage Centre, 354
Castlehill, The Royal Mile, Edinburgh
Tel : 0131 220 0441
Open all year

IRELAND
Old Bushmills Distillery, Bushmills, County
Antrim BT57 8XH, Northern Ireland
Tel: 0801 2657 31521
www.irish-whiskey-trail.com
Open April to October, Mon–Sat
9.30am–5.30pm; Sun 12noon–5.30pm
Last tour 4pm
November to March, Mon–Fri every hour
from 10.30am–3.30pm
Free comparative tasting, bar, restaurant and
shop

Old Midleton Distillery, Distillery Walk,
Midleton County Cork, Republic of Ireland
Tel: +353 216 13591
www.jameson.ie
Open all year. March to October, tours every
day, from 10am–6pm. Last tour 4pm
November to February, Mon–Fri noon and
3pm; Sat & Sun 2pm and 4pm
Free comparative tasting, bar, restaurant and
shop

Old Jameson
Distillery, Bow St,
Smithfield Village,
Dublin 7, Republic
of Ireland
Tel: +353 180
72355
www.jameson.ie
Open all year
(except Dec 25th
and Good Friday)
9.30am–6pm Last
tour 5pm
Free comparative
tasting, bar,
restaurant and shop

Tullamore Dew Heritage Centre
Tullamore, County Offaly, Republic of
Ireland
www.tullamore-dew.com
Open all year. May to September
9.00am–6.00pm; October to April
10.00am–5.00pm. Sundays all year
noon–5.00pm
Cafe, licensed restaurnat, shop

Cooley
Locke's Distillery Museum
Kilbeggan, County, Westmeath, Republic of
Ireland
Tel: +353 506 32134
www.cooleywhiskey.com
Open April to October 9am–6pm; November
to March, 10am–4pm
Museum, exhibition and café

USA
Jim Beam American Outpost
149 Happy Hollow Road
Clermont, KY
Tel: +1 502 543 9877
Tours Mon–Sat 9am–4.30pm
Sun 1pm–4pm
Closed major holidays
Museum and shop

Wild Turkey
US Hwy 62 E,
Lawrenceburg, KY
Tel: +1 502 839 4544
Tours Mon–Fri 9am, 10.30am, 12.30pm,
2.30pm
Closed major holidays
Shop and café

Maker's Mark
3350 Burks Spring Road
Loretto, KY
Tel: +1 502 865 2099
Tours Mon–Sat 10.30am–3.30pm
Sun 1.30pm, 2.30pm, 3.30pm
Closed major holidays
Shop

Four Roses
1224 Bonds Mill Road
Lawrenceburg, KY
Tel: +1 502 839 3436
Tours by appointment only

Labrot & Graham
7885 McCracken Pike
Versailles, KY
Tel: +1 606 879 1812
Tours 11am, 1pm, 2pm, 3pm
Closed major holidays
Museum, shop

Buffalo Trace
1001 Wilkinson Boulevard
Leestown, Frankfort, KY
Tel: +1 502 696 5926
Tours Mon–Fri 9am–2pm
Museum, café and shop

Heaven Hill
1064 Loretto Road
Bardstown, KY
Tel: +1 502 348 3921
Tours Mon–Fri 10.30am and 2.30pm, by
prior arrangement only

Barton
Not open to the public

Jack Daniels
PO Box 199 Highway 55

Lynchburg, Tennessee 37352
Tel: +1 931 759 4221
Open all year 8am–4pm
Admission free
Museum, café and shopping

George A Dickel Cascade Distillery
PO Box 490, 1950 Cascade Hollow Road
Tullahoma, Tennessee 37388
Tel: +1 931 857 857 3124
Open: All year, Mon–Fri 9am–3pm
Admission free
Museum, café, shopping

Oscar Getz Whiskey Museum
Spalding Hall,
114 North Fifth Street, Bardstown, KY
40004
Tel: +1 502 348 2999
Highly recommended

CANADA
Walkerville Distillery (Canadian Club)
2072 Riverside Drive E,
Windsor, ON N8Y 4S5
Tel:+1 519 254 5171
www.canadianclubwhisky.com
Open all year
Free tours

Kittling Ridge
Grimsby, Ontario
Tel: +1 905 945 9225
www.kittlingridge.com
Free tastings 7 days a week, all year.
Tours June to September only Tues–Fri 2pm;
weekends and holidays, 11am & 2pm

All details correct at time of going to press.

GLOSSARY

ABV (Alcohol by volume) The alcoholic strength of the spirit measured as a percentage part of the total volume of liquid – eg, 40%ABV is 40 per cent alcohol, 60 per cent water. See *Proof*

Age statement The age on a bottle always refers to the youngest component in the blend/vatting.

Backset (US) (or setback, or sour mash) The acidic residue from the first distillation which is added to the mash tub and/or the fermenter, totalling no less than 25 per cent of the overall mash. Used to stop bacterial infection and to lower the pH in the fermenter, allowing even fermentation.

Batch distillation (or pot still, or discontinuous distillation) The first distillation produces a low-strength spirit which is then redistilled (sometimes twice) and separated into three parts – heads, heart and tails. Only the heart is retained.

Beer (North America) Fermented mash. See *Wash*

Beer still (US) The first still used in the distillation process – usually a single column still.

Blending The mixing of different types of spirit (eg rye, Bourbon or malt) with grain whisky. In Canada a blend may also contain 9.09% of other mature imported spirits, wines or distilled fruit juices.

Blended whiskey (US) A minimum 20 per cent straight whiskey, blended with neutral spirit.

Blended whisky (Scotland) A blend of grain and malt whiskies.

Bourbon US whiskey made from a mash of no less than 51 per cent corn, distilled to a maximum strength of 80%ABV and aged in new charred oak casks.

Charcoal mellowing (or The Lincoln County Process) Used in Tennessee, where the new spirit is filtered through beds of charcoal before being put into barrel.

Charring Firing the inside of a barrel. The flame opens up cracks in the surface of the oak, allowing easy penetration by the spirit, and releases sugar compounds to aid flavouring and colouring of the spirit.

Chill filtration A filtering process, by lowering the temperature of the spirit to remove compounds which could cause clouding. Also removes some congeners.

Column still (or continuous, Coffey or beer still) Works by forcing pressurised steam up the column, where it meets the descending alcoholic wash, vapourising the alcohol and carrying it up to be condensed.

Condenser Apparatus which turns the alcoholic vapours into liquid form. Traditionally this was a spiral of copper immersed in cold water. See *Worm tub*

Congeners Chemical compounds found in a spirit, formed during fermentation, distillation and maturation. They contain many flavour-carrying elements. The higher the alcoholic strength of a spirit, the fewer its congeners.

Cut (Scotland) The middle fraction of the distillate which is saved is called the cut. The impure alcohols are called foreshots and feints.

Distillation The extraction of alcohol from a fermented liquid, by heating it. Because alcohol boils at a lower strength than water, the vapour can be collected and condensed, thus concentrating the strength.

Doubler (North America) A domed pot still, used for the second distillation.

Draff (Scotland) Animal feed, made from the spent grains after mashing is complete.

Enzymes Organic catalysts which convert non-fermentable starches into fermentable soluble sugars. Grains such as malted barley and rye contain these enzymes and are added to other cereal crops for this conversion, or saccharification.

Esters Flavour-giving chemical compounds. Produced by the reaction of alcohol and acids during fermentation and maturation, and appear soon after the start of distillation.

Feints (Scotland/Ireland) (or Tails/Low Wines) Unwanted end part of the second distillation. These are high in undesirable congeners, low in alcohol and are collected and redistilled.

Fermenters Large vessels made of steel or wood, for turning the mash into beer or wash.

Foreshots See *Heads*

Fusel oil A heavy congener.

Grain whisky A high-strength, delicately flavoured whisky, usually made from corn (or wheat) in a continuous still.

Grist Barley that has been ground into a rough flour, prior to mashing.

Heads (or Foreshots) Volatile first runnings

from the still during the second distillation. These are collected and redistilled along with the feints and wash/beer.

Kilning Process of arresting the germination of malted barley through heat – sometimes involving peat fires.

Lyne arm (or lie pipe) The arm that leads from the top of the neck of a pot still to the condenser, the angle of which can affect the amount of reflux in a spirit.

Malt

1) A grain, usually barley but also rye, which has been stimulated artificially into germination and then halted by drying. (A process known as 'Malting'. The malt is high in sugars and enzymes.

2) Common term for a single malt whisky – a whisky made exclusively from malted barley and distilled at least twice in a pot still.

Maltings Buildings used for malting.

Marrying Process whereby recently blended spirits are placed in a large vat before bottling. Allows the different distillates to homogenise.

Mash The sweet liquid produced after hot water has been flushed through the base ingredient in the mash tub/tun. This extracts the fermentable sugars which are converted to maltose by enzyme activity, prior to fermentation.

Mashbill (North America) The percentage makeup of ingredients (corn, wheat, rye, barley) in mashing.

Mouth-feel Shape and texture of the spirit in the mouth when tasted.

New make The young spirit, fresh from the still.

Nose The aroma of a spirit.

Oak The most common type of wood in casks used for maturation. Oak is strong and watertight, allowing light oxidation. It also imparts a range of colour and flavour components to the maturing spirit. Different types of oak give different effects.

Peat A soft fuel made from compressed and carbonised vegetable matter – usually heather, wood, grass and occasionally seaweed. Its smoke, known as peat reek, is very pungent and when used in drying malted barley gives malt a phenolic aroma.

Pot still Stills used in batch distillation.

Proof American measurement of alcoholic strength. A 100° proof spirit is 50 %ABV.

Rectification Purification of a distillate by redistillation, giving a high-strength distillate with very few congeners.

Reflux Process in which the shape or control of a still forces alcoholic vapours back down the still, to be redistilled. High levels of reflux tend to produce a lighter spirit.

Ricks Wooden frames to hold maturing American whiskey.

Rye whiskey Whiskey made from a minimum 51per cent rye.

Single malt whisky A malt whisky from a single distillery.

Sour mash Another term for backset. A sour mash whiskey must contain 25 per cent backset. All Kentucky and Tennessee whiskey is sour mash.

Spirit still The second (or third) still used in pot still distillation.

Thumper A type of doubler containing water, through which alcoholic vapours pass.

Toasting Process of lightly heating the inside of a barrel, releasing sugars in the wood. A more gentle process than charring.

Vatting (Scotland/Ireland) The mixing together of malts from one or more distilleries.

Vatted malt A blend of malts from more than one distillery.

Wash (or Distillers Beer) Fermented liquid, ready to be distilled.

Washback Scottish term for fermenter.

Wash still The first (and usually larger) still used in pot still distillation.

Worm The coiled copper condensing tube that winds around the inside of the worm tub.

Worm tub An old form of condenser, consisting of a vat of cold water containing a worm.

Yeast A micro-organism of the fungi family which feeds on sugar, converting it to alcohol and CO_2. Also imparts flavour compounds to the liquid.

INDEX

ACKNOWLEDGEMENTS

Allied Domecq Spirits & Wine Ltd 53, 74-75, 96-97, 98-99, 112 Top, 112 Bottom, 113, 142, 143 Top, 143 Bottom **Austin Nichols & Co. Inc.** 122, 123 left, 123 right **Barton Brands Ltd.** 134 Top, 134 Bottom, 135 Top, 135 Bottom **Brown-Forman Corporation** 136-137 **Ben Nevis Distillery** 65 Top/ Alex Gillespie Photography 65 Bottom Left, 65 Bottom Right **Dave Broom** Back cover centre, Back cover right, 6 Top, 10 Top, 10 Centre, 11 Top Left, 18 Top Right, 44 right, 58 Top Right, 59, 69 Bottom, 77 Top, 78 Bottom, 85 Top **Buffalo Trace** 130 right, 130 Top, 130 Bottom, 131 left **Campbell Distillers** 38-39, 58 Centre **Cooley Distillers Plc.** 114 left, 114-115 Bottom, 116 left, 116 right, 117 **Cutty Sark International** 28, 95 Centre **John Dewar & Sons Ltd** 102 **Kintyre Photography**/ Stuart Andrew 81 Bottom **The Edrington Group** 9 Top, 9 Centre, 63 Top, 63 Centre Left, 94, 95 Top, 95 Bottom **Glenmorangie Plc.** 20-21, 24-25, 78 Top, 79 **Octopus Publishing Group Ltd.** /Leigh Jones Back Cover background, title, 4-5, 12, 62, 63 Bottom, 104-105, 147 Top /Mark Winwood Front Cover left, Front Cover right, Front Cover background, Front cover centre left, Front cover centre right, half title, 86-87, 118-119, 140-141 **Heaven Hill Distillery Inc.** 7 right, 11 Centre Right, 132, 132 right, 132 Bottom Right, 133 **Highland Distillers Brands Ltd.** 14-15, 36-37, 43, 60-61, 70-71 **Irish Distillers Limited** Back Cover centre left, 6 Bottom, 7 left, 10 Top Left, 106 Top Right, 106 Centre Left, 107, 108 left, 108-109 Bottom, 109, 110, 110 Top Right, 110 Centre **Inver House Distillers** 16-17, 22, 30 **Invergordon Distillers** 82 **J&G Grant** 46-47 **JBB Plc.** 68, 69 Top **Jim Beam Brands Co.** 120-121 **Kittling Ridge Ltd.** 146, 147 Bottom **Labrot & Graham Distillers Co.** 128 Centre Left, 128 Bottom Right, 129 Top, 129 Centre Right **Morrison Bowmore Distillers Ltd.** 52, 72-73, 83 **Maker's Mark Distillery Inc.** 124, 124 right, 125 Top, 125 Bottom **The Royal Commission on the Ancient & Historical Monuments of Scotland** 42 **Seagram** 26, 26 Bottom, 27 Top, 27 Bottom, 29, 50 Top, 50 Bottom, 51 Top, 51 Bottom, 100, 101 Top, 101 Bottom, 126-127, 144-145 **Springbank Distillery Ltd.** 80, 81 Top **United Distillers & Vintners** 9 Bottom, 18-19, 23, 31, 40-41, 44 left, 45, 48-49, 54-55, 56-57, 64, 66-67, 76, 77 Bottom, 84, 85 right, 85 Centre, 88, 89 Top Right, 89 Bottom, 90 Top Left, 91 Top Left, 91 Top Right, 92 left, 92 Bottom, 93 Top, 93 Bottom, 138-139 **William Grant & Sons International Ltd.** 7 Top, 10 Bottom, 11 Top Right, 11 Centre Left, 32-33, 34-35, 103 right, 103 Bottom Left

Hamlyn would like to thank **Oddbins Ltd** for providing much needed bottles of whisky for use in this book.

This book is about whisky people and couldn't have been written without the help of a huge number of folk around the world who have been enormously generous with their time. Their love for their job and passion for their craft shines in the bottles we all enjoy. There isn't enough space to thank them all, but particular thanks must go to: Jim McEwan for sowing the seed and the guys at Bowmore for allowing me to work there, Christine Logan; John Ramsay, David Robertson, Hamish Proctor, Simon Lyons, Bill Farrar, Dominique Anderson; Jim Cryle, Denis Malcolm, Alan Greig, Colin Scott, Rachael Dutton; Lucy Pritchard, Nick Morgan, Mike Nicolson, Peter Warren, David Hardy, Angie Mackay, Kenny Bain, Iain MacArthur, Mike Gunn, Turnbull Hutton, Christine Wright and Ian Grieve; Bill Lumsden, Cathy Law, Stuart and Jackie Thomson, Graham Eunson, Ed Dodson; Alan Winchester, John Reid, Charlotte Fraser, Vanessa Wright; Robert Hicks, Sandy Hyslop, Iain Henderson, Bill Bergius; David Hume, David Stewart; Colin Ross, Euan Mitchell, Mhairi Adam, Malcolm Waring, Willie Tait; Eily Kilgannon, David Quinn, Barry Crockett and Barry Walsh and Brendan Monks; David Hynes; Jimmy Russell, Bill Samuels, Dave Backus, Chris McCrory, Ken and Jackie Hoskins, Booker Noe, Jerry Dalton, Parker Beam, Bill Creason, Bill Friel, Ken Pierce, Mike Booth, Art Peterson and John Hall
Special thanks to Dr Herzog for his palate, Boris for the Lagavulin photo, Poppy for keeping me going and Andy Sparrow for putting decent drams on BA.
Marcin Miller and all at Whisky Magazine, Nick Faith and all at the International Spirits Challenge, Charlie McLean, Michael Jackson, Jonathan Goodall, Chris Losh, Fiona Sims and my noble fellow smuggler Chris Orr.
To my editors: Nina Sharman for making the brave decision to try something slightly different; Tarda Davison-Aitkins for his Zen-like calm when everyone was losing the plot; and to Rosie Garai for her wonderful work on the picture research.
Finally to my lovely wife, Jo, for yet again coping with a crazed writer and for being a constant and loving source of support.

Dedicated to Les and Douglas
Gus an Bris an Là!